D0324930

WITHDRAWN
LEASIDE BRANCH

Baby Is a Four-Letter Word

Surviving the First Two Years of Parenthood

Dorianne Sager

with a foreword by Ann Douglas

KEY PORTER BOOKS

Library and Archives Canada Cataloguing in Publication

Sager, Dorianne
    Baby Is a four-letter word : surviving the first two years of parenthood / Dorianne Sager ; with a foreword by Ann Douglas.

ISBN 1-55263-751-4

1. Parenting—Humor. 2. Infants—Humor. 3. Canadian wit and humor (English). I. Title.

PN6231.P2S25 2006   C818'.602   C2005-906553-2

THE CANADA COUNCIL | LE CONSEIL DES ARTS
FOR THE ARTS | DU CANADA
SINCE 1957 | DEPUIS 1957

ONTARIO ARTS COUNCIL
CONSEIL DES ARTS DE L'ONTARIO

The publisher gratefully acknowledges the support of the Canada Council for the Arts and the Ontario Arts Council for its publishing program. We acknowledge the support of the Government of Ontario through the Ontario Media Development Corporation's Ontario Book Initiative.

We acknowledge the financial support of the Government of Canada through the Book Publishing Industry Development Program (BPIDP) for our publishing activities.

Key Porter Books Limited
Six Adelaide Street East, Tenth Floor
Toronto, Ontario
Canada M5C 1H6

www.keyporter.com

Text design: Marijke Friesen
Illustrations: Francis Blake

Printed and bound in Canada

06 07 08 09 10 6 5 4 3 2 1

To my family—
because we all need someone to blame

—Acknowledgements—

Parts of this book first appeared—in an abridged format—in the *Vancouver Sun* and I would like to give a special thanks to Patricia Graham, editor-in-chief, who believed in me enough to give me my own column. And to all the parents who faithfully read the column and shared my tears and laughter each week—you gave me the confidence to turn my stories into a book.

Warmest thanks to all my friends who are parents who offered encouragement, inspiration and priceless material. To Sally Harding, my agent—a Kiwi in exile like my husband—for her faith and guidance; to Linda Pruessen at Key Porter Books, for bringing me into the fold, and to Ann Douglas, who took time out of an already hectic schedule to write the foreword. Also, my sister Sheri, who claims I made my editor's job easy because I forced her to read every chapter at least five times before handing it in. And to my parents, who deny every quotation in the book (but did, in fact, say every one)—you gave me my sense of humour.

But especially to Andrew, whom I will never be able to thank enough for all those hours spent with Zach at the train museum, the aquarium and walking the seawall—all so I could have some time alone to write. You are my hero. And of course, my darling little Zach, the true creator of this book. I never would have been able to do it without you (and the espresso machine!).

Thank you.

—Contents—

Fuelled by Love, Powered by Caffeine

It only took me about fifteen seconds to become a member of the Dorianne Sager Fan Club—and I may have been a little slow on the uptake because I was fiddling with my cup of coffee. I mean, *really*, what's *not* to admire about a mother who is capable of inventing her own toddler toys by twisting together coffee cup lids, straws, stir sticks, and other random bits of coffee house paraphernalia—and of coming up with enough different variations on the coffee house–toy theme to keep a toddler entertained throughout an hour-long interview?

Wait a second. I'd better set the record straight before I get Dorianne into major hot water with the Motherhood Police—that gang of self-appointed do-gooders who wait for the rest of us mere mom-mortals to slip up. Dorianne may be a highly skilled journalist but I can assure you that she wasn't intending to subject the toddler in question to an hour-long interrogation, entertaining or otherwise. It's simply not her style. Besides, the Canadian Pediatric Society must have a policy against prolonged toddler interviews—and if they don't, then surely Dr. Phil does.

So you can relax: no toddlers were interviewed on this particular occasion. I was the one on the receiving end of all of the questions. You see, Dorianne was interviewing me for her popular *Vancouver Sun* "Baby Steps" parenting column while I was in town promoting one of my books. And, having first-hand knowledge of just how well coffee and motherhood mix, she had suggested that I meet her and her famous toddler son Zach at a local coffeehouse so that we could talk motherhood over mugs of mother fuel. (Zach, as I recall, had opted for BYOB—bring your own bottle. Or maybe it was bring your own sippy cup. I can't quite recall.)

Before my coffee was even cool enough to start sipping, Dorianne had totally won me over.

I liked the way she was able to scoop Zach up in seconds whenever he tried to make a bolt out the door—all without missing a beat in the conversation.

I liked the fact that she was frank and honest and funny—that she was determined to tell the truth about motherhood *as it really is* rather than trying to serve up some tired Hollywood rendition of how motherhood is supposed to be.

I liked the fact that she didn't get all frazzled and freaked out when Zach had a minor meltdown. Her attitude was one of, "This is me. This is my kid. We're kind of a package deal."

I think you'll take an instant liking to Dorianne Sager as you make your way through the pages of this frank and funny book. You'll see that she understands that parenting requires a robust sense of humour, a ready supply of caffeine, instant access to the mommy-and-daddy grapevine (the only known antidote to the lifetime membership in Club Anxiety that you acquired the moment you became a parent), a reduced need for sleep (or at least the ability to hoodwink yourself into believing that you don't need as much sleep), and the ability to love your child with total, dizzying abandon.

Dorianne says she hopes that you will treat her book as "a license to confide with another mother"—that you'll give yourself permission to truly open up to another mom by admitting that you could use some advice, information, moral support—and perhaps even another cup of coffee.

—Ann Douglas
www.motherofallblogs.com

Ann Douglas is the author and creator of The Mother of All book series and The Mother of All Solutions series, and the mother of four children, ages eight through eighteen.

Declining Birth Rate?

Don't Believe Everything You Read

Never let the media—or your mother—influence your sex life. According to the newspaper headlines, infertility had reached epidemic proportions. According to the experts, a woman's fertility starts declining in her late twenties and with each passing year it plummets faster than Nortel's share price. According to my mother, I wasn't getting any younger. The message was clear. I was thirty; my eggs were numbered.

My thirtieth birthday was not so much a milestone—my reward for surviving my twenties—as a best-before date. One day I was living in London, England, with my husband, Andrew, enjoying a carefree life as a journalist; writing groundbreaking features on the sex lives of celebrities and the season's top ten lipsticks. I was networking at fancy press parties, drinking champagne in the office and being sent to interview Colin Firth. The next, I was buying a basal body thermometer and charting my cervical mucus, afraid that the whole act of baby-making might take years and here we were wasting time with selfish sex for pleasure.

And so began our quest for parenthood, not because I was feeling particularly maternal—I hadn't even plugged in my biological clock, but apparently it was ticking anyway. No, it was the threat of reproductive organs with an expiry date that pushed us into unprotected copulation.

Like I said, never let the media influence your sex life. A consultation with a fertility expert and an ovulation predictor kit is not always a prerequisite to getting pregnant once you hit thirty; sometimes just being in the same room is all you need. If we had known the first egg out of the gate was going to be the winner we wouldn't have tried as hard. So now I was thirty, pregnant, still in the middle of forging a career and completely unprepared for how this baby was about to change our lives. We left London for Vancouver, bought a house, bought a car, started a new business and had a baby. Our son, Zach, is now two-and-a-half years old and Andrew and I are still recovering.

And we aren't the only ones. Once we got pregnant it seemed like all my friends were popping buns in the oven faster than a baker on speed. So much for flagging fertility. We seem to be in the middle of a baby boom and motherhood has become our new career. We are all in our early to mid-thirties, but we're carting around bodies that feel like they've aged twenty years overnight. Some are still struggling with professional goals that have been put on hold, some are dealing with the pressures of supporting a family, while others are optimistic that they can continue to work, travel, dine out and live like they always have (they're the ones that are still pregnant). We spend more on baby clothes and accessories than our parents did on their first car; our purses hold baby wipes and teething rings instead of condoms and lipstick; our DVD collection has been overrun by *Baby Einstein*; and we catch ourselves muttering, "What the hell were we thinking?" Sleep deprived and, let's face it, slightly heavier than we once were, we are completely shell-shocked by our new lives.

No one ever tells you that while you can spend nine months preparing for parenthood, you won't have a clue what to do with the baby once it actually arrives. Somewhere between the birth canal and the delivery room the instruction manual gets lost and you're just supposed to *know* how to be a parent. Luckily, everyone else around you is an expert, and you soon find yourself fielding advice from family, in-laws, doctors, friends, the lady at the grocery store and the pizza delivery guy.

But this book is different. I don't have any expert parenting advice to give. If I did, I would be sleeping more than four hours a night. What I *do* have to offer is the ability to laugh about these early years: the endless crying, the pails of dirty diapers, the pains of breast-feeding, the effects of sleep deprivation and the peaks of utter helplessness and pure joy that make up the mess of motherhood. Besides, no amount of information can ever prepare you for life with a baby. Despite having read just about every how-to parenting book on the market, I never knew that, when changing a gassy infant, "the shit hitting the fan" is not, in fact, a cliché, but an occupational hazard. Or, that the only time you will project breast milk across a room is when you are in a crowded public space, trying to nurse discreetly. There are some things you get to discover all on your own.

I first started writing about my misadventures with parenthood in the column "Baby Steps" for the *Vancouver Sun*. My stories drew on the absurdities of motherhood, had no real journalistic merit, and were simply tales of another parent's struggles to cope. I was absolutely floored by the response the column provoked from mothers, fathers, even grandparents, who thanked me for giving them the chance to enjoy the humour that is to be found amid the chaos of parenting. It was quite a relief. I had thought that I was alone in my journey, that the demands of my over-energetic son, a sex life gone AWOL, and the constant anxiety over whether I was screwing everything up was driving me to the nuthouse. Little did I realize that I was sitting in bumper-to-bumper traffic with other parents, all headed in the same direction.

I remember a dad who e-mailed me in response to my sleep deprivation article to let me know about his experience with his daughter. "I clearly remember the morning I woke up and said: 'She didn't wake up!'" he wrote. "She had just turned five. Which may be why the age difference between her and her brother is five years and nine months." Every now and then I think of that exhausted father and remind my husband that we only have two-and-a-half more years to go.

Another father, an aviation safety inspector, wrote to me about my piece on flying with a toddler. He was about to venture on a long-haul trip to Europe with his two young children for the first time, and while he hoped I was exaggerating about my experience (I wish I had been) he did let me know that the only person he knew of who had received a lifetime ban from flying was travelling with a live pig who got loose in the cabin. I was lucky, the only animal I was travelling with was a wild fifteen-month-old—so my son and I should be allowed back on a plane again very soon.

A great-grandmother also wrote me a lovely letter about my article on discipline, assuring me that, based on her own experiences raising children, my strong-willed toddler would turn out just fine. She also said that the next time my son had a tantrum I should take him by the ankles and lift him upside down to stop the screaming. It had been suggested to her by a psychologist at the University of British Columbia when she was a young mother, which just goes to show you shouldn't believe everything you're told about parenting. Besides, I tried it. It doesn't work.

I even received a letter of congratulations from the head of an international organization for (purposely) childless couples. While I was more than a little suspicious of his warm words of praise, it was clear that even people who had decided not to have children (but who had lost friends to parenthood), could relate to what I was writing about.

I never imagined that my funny and honest reflections of life with a baby would soon become a lifeline to many mothers as they chuckled over the highs and lows we all experience. It's funny. Even though we're more informed and prepared for motherhood than any other generation before us, we still seem to have been caught utterly by surprise. Perhaps it's because we were brought up to believe we could do anything; that motherhood could be conquered—just like the professional or academic worlds where many of us had excelled. We never imagined that a baby would be cheeky enough to tell us any different. And even though we have all discovered parenthood to be an ultimately rewarding experience, it remains, as one mother said, "the craziest thing I've ever done while sober."

I also discovered that although I made a point of not offering advice, I got plenty in return. Parenthood is a hot topic. Like religion, sex or politics, whenever you bring it up you risk coming across as either too conservative, too liberal or just plain perverse. While many parents could relate to my experiences, I had others who would contact me to point out the obvious flaws in my parenting skills—which annoyed my mother to no end, since it left her temporarily out of a job. (And just for the record, when I wrote about the parallels of raising a child and training a dog, I never meant to insult pit bulls.) But while everyone has their opinions about child rearing, the one thing we all share in common is the need to laugh, at ourselves and our children. Surviving this job requires a good sense of humour—or a good supply of Valium.

Laughter is what keeps us going when the realities of parenthood start to feel overwhelming, and that is why I've written this book.

So to all parents—expectant or new, young or old, experienced or fumbling—*Baby Is a Four-Letter Word* is for you. Treat this collection of short stories about these precious early years of parenthood as a license to confide with another mother. Allow yourself the chance to laugh, to cry and to share in the demands of parenting. Life with a baby may be rewarding, but it is also fraught with loneliness and anxiety. And while I may not be able to pass on any advice, I can tell you that you are not alone, and you are not crazy—no matter how hard your baby is working to convince you otherwise.

Parenthood. It's a precarious, exhilarating, heartbreaking, frustrating, hilarious ride. And even though I'm in no way qualified to be on this roller coaster, I'm still glad I've got my ticket.

—*Dorianne Sager*

Part 1
Welcome to the Jungle

—1—

You Call This a Plan?

Learning to Live with a Newborn

"Planned parenthood" must be a misnomer. Sure, we planned to have a baby. I remember it distinctly: it was the last time Andrew and I had sex without worrying about bumping into the baby or waking the baby. We bought nursery furniture, chose a name, signed up for childbirth classes. *We planned.* But from the moment our baby poked his head into the world, absolutely nothing has gone as planned.

In my first trimester I decided to take a hypnobirthing course so I could overcome my fear of labour. I desperately clung to the instructor's assurance that this self-hypnosis method could guarantee an "often pain-free" birth—especially since every mother I had spoken to assured me that childbirth was going to be "almost definitely excruciating." But I was in luck. The following nine months of positive visualization, breathing exercises and calming music somehow helped me transcend my naturally high-strung state, and my son Zach was born in three blissfully short, albeit slightly uncomfortable, drug-free hours.

And then it all went pear-shaped. My body—so completely unfamiliar with this state of relaxation—took onboard the "let everything go" mantra that my hypnobirthing tape kept repeating and my uterus decided to go on a field trip. I discovered "often pain-free" *didn't* include passing a uterus—and it most certainly didn't apply to shoving one back in.

Without warning, my amazing and serene birth experience flipped over to a terrifying episode of *ER*. The dimmed lights were slammed on in full force as a team of doctors rushed in to take centre stage, shouting out directions and casting my midwife and nurse into the background to watch the show like a pair of extras. The sense of celebration that followed Zach's birth turned to one of panic and chaos. "Am I going to die?" I whispered to my husband, and the fear in his eyes told me that his reassurances were more for his benefit than mine. "Get this woman into the OR! Now!" I heard someone yell just before I passed out from the pain and shock. Suddenly, my introduction to motherhood—the moment I had lived for everyday for nine months—became the moment I lived through.

But a wayward uterus wasn't the only thing I hadn't "planned" on. I never planned to come home from the hospital with milk ducts so engorged that it looked like two camels had parked under my armpits. I never planned on a year of broken sleep. I never planned on flashing my bare breasts to strangers on a plane, in a restaurant or a shopping mall because I couldn't figure out how to get my baby to latch on discreetly. I never planned on feeling so unqualified for motherhood. And I never planned on wiping poo stains off my walls.

Living with a baby is learning to live with chaos. For women who like an ordered household, the mess can be unnerving. The day we brought our new son home from the hospital was the last day I ever saw my coffee table. The bouquets of fresh flowers and stylishly piled magazines lasted long enough for me to say, "The house looks gorgeous." Within a half an hour, a vase of flowers had been knocked over by the diaper bag and the magazines were on the floor—replaced with piles of diapers, baby wipes, my breast pump, a breast-feeding manual, a notepad to record how many diapers the baby went through each hour and a takeout box of pizza.

Months passed before I could sit on my beautiful, completely impractical, custom designed couches with my baby without covering them with blankets first. Despite my best efforts, every piece of furniture we own has been christened with some sort of baby stain. I have a closet full of designer clothes but I spend every day in my track suit. It's the only thing that goes with smeared Farley's biscuits. My life has turned into an endless spin cycle: feeding the baby, burping the baby, changing the baby, cooking, cleaning and laundry. Loads and loads of laundry.

There's no point resisting the chaos a baby brings into your life. I remember the moment I first realized I was a parent. It wasn't when I held my son in my arms for the first time. It was over breakfast one morning with my husband. I had dried poo all over my sleeve from a particularly disturbing encounter with a projectile bowel movement, (never try to change a diaper in the dark) and Andrew had fresh vomit on his knee and shoulder from burping Zach. Yet, there we were, sitting blissfully at the table, drinking coffee and reading the newspaper, as if this were a totally normal way to exist.

Babies don't arrive with a disclaimer that warns parents just how drastically their lives are about to change. And who would believe it if they did? A baby doesn't have the power to turn your world upside down, you tell yourself. And you're right—a baby has the power to knock it right off its axis. And still, couples put more thought and research into decisions like what kind of car to buy. As romantic notions of parenthood take hold, the decision to have a child is often cemented with a simple question: "Hey, want to open another bottle of wine?" The in-depth conversation about whether you were really ready to start a family comes much later—usually at three in the morning, when your nightgown is soaked because your breasts are spurting like a burst water main, you haven't slept in days, the only noise you can hear above the din of your baby's desperate wailing is your husband's snoring and you scream out into the darkness, "I didn't sign up for this!"

No, you can't plan for parenthood. It's like a pit of quicksand; you've sunk halfway down before you even realize you've stepped in it. But then you see your baby smile, or take his first step, and the intensity of emotion that pours out of you makes you feel vulnerable and exhilarated all at the same time. Your house is a mess and your heart is splayed on the floor eating week-old Cheerios. You can't plan for that. You just have to enjoy it.

2

Boob Job

The Joys of Breast-feeding

For me, the decision to breast-feed was an easy one, not necessarily because I believe breast milk is always best. As a rule, I try to avoid getting involved in the politics of breast-feeding and the whole debate over whether breast-fed babies are healthier and smarter. I was a formula baby and my husband was breast-fed, and I don't need to give my mother-in-law any more ammunition. No, for me it was purely about convenience. Breast-feeding didn't require carrying any extra baggage, other than the pregnancy fat that wouldn't shift. There was no refrigeration required, no sterilizing, no measuring, *no problem*. I had two breasts and a baby, how hard could it be? Except that it took three nurses, my midwife and a lactation consultant to teach me how to hold my breast and my baby at the same time. It was weeks before I could line up my nipple with Zach's mouth without first poking him in the eye.

Breast-feeding *should* come naturally, but like childbirth, it doesn't come to you without a small degree of discomfort. All the "experts" will tell you that breast-feeding is not supposed to hurt, but, hey, gums aren't supposed to be sharp. Try attaching something to your breast that has stronger suction than your average vacuum cleaner without flinching.

A proper latch is the key to successful breast-feeding—if it's wrong, it feels like your baby is drawing broken glass out of your nipple instead of milk. But getting your baby to latch on properly is about as easy as finding a fat-free chocolate dessert that's worth eating. My midwife taught me how to sandwich my breast tissue together so the entire nipple and most of the areola could fit inside my baby's mouth. Just between you and me, I made enough nipple sandwiches to start my own deli before I finally got the hang of it.

And then I discovered I had Raynaud's syndrome. My nipples would blanch and burn after a feeding or when they got cold—all of which made winter, breast-feeding and shopping in the frozen food aisle unbearable. Luckily, a miracle ointment cured that—just before my son's first two teeth appeared and my nipple sandwiches took on a whole new appeal. Yet, despite the pain, whenever my son would turn lovingly towards me, his little gums bared like a piranha setting in for the kill, I would wince and think, "You just can't get this kind of moment with a bottle."

When mothers talk about the bonding experience of nursing, they are really referring to the fact that their baby is always attached. Life as a twenty-four-hour buffet is exhausting, and unless you can find yourself a wet nurse, there are no substitute waiters or menu alternatives. I still remember the first time my husband left me and Zach on our own for a whole day, not long after Zach was born. He said goodbye in the morning and I waved from the couch where I was sitting nursing, with the TV humming in the background. He returned eight hours later to find me in the exact same position. "Did you do anything today?" he asked incredulously.

I was galled at his insensitivity. "Did I do anything today?" I repeated to myself. Hell, I was impressed that, in between the seemingly endless feedings, I had managed to make it to the bathroom—twice! I even remembered to brush my teeth during one trip. "What?" I replied. "He's still alive isn't he?"

Fortunately, once you finally do get the hang of nursing it becomes second nature. I got to the point where I was so familiar with having my breasts pummelled, scratched, bitten and sucked dry that I barely even noticed if they were flapping about uncovered like hanging laundry on a breezy day. "For God's sake," my sister said to me once. "Will you please put them away, we're at the mall!"

I soon forgot all the advice in my breast-feeding pamphlets, like how you should nurse in a quiet, relaxed atmosphere, or avoid drinking anything hot while nursing lest it spill onto the baby, because I was too busy making dinner, answering the door, grocery shopping, crossing the street—all with my little appendage happily sucking away. I learned to ignore the disapproving glances of women who wouldn't touch a drop of alcohol or caffeine while they were breast-feeding because it might unsettle the baby. Walking past the crib could unsettle my baby, so I figured I might as well have a glass of wine in my hand. And I laughed off the suggestion to pin a ribbon to my bra strap so I would know which side I finished on. Instead, I considered pinning my name and address to my breast because after the first few months of nursing I couldn't remember who I was or where I lived.

The barometer for what passes as normal changes immensely once you've pushed an eight-pound baby out of your body. Having your breasts hooked up to an electronic milking machine while you chat with friends becomes normal. So does flashing your breasts to complete strangers as you latch on a squirming, screaming infant. And don't worry about the times when your baby pushes your breast away with surprising force and you squirt milk on your furniture, or the couple celebrating their anniversary at the table beside you in a packed restaurant. It's all normal.

As heartwarming as moments like that can be, there will come a time when you decide to wean. I am a strong advocate of breast-feeding, but even I was getting worried when at fourteen months, Zach was lifting up my top looking for breakfast. I decided if my baby was old enough to open the refrigerator door, he was old enough to get his own milk.

But now that Zach leaves teeth marks on his sippy cup instead of me, I find myself missing the days when I was the only one who could nourish him, when he depended on me so completely. It may be a struggle, it may be painful and exhausting, but breast-feeding is still the most rewarding boob job you will ever have.

3

You Can Sleep When You're Dead

The Effects of Sleep Deprivation, Part I

I glanced at the calendar hanging on the fridge. "Our son is fifteen months old today," I said to Andrew, passing him a cup of coffee. "And we've been awake to enjoy every minute of it."

Anyone who has children will tell you to savour the early years of babyhood because they go by so quickly. Well, when your day isn't broken up by eight hours of sleep every night, time doesn't actually move all that fast.

Before I became a parent I used to dread hanging out with friends who were. It seemed like all adult conversation stopped and everyone would just sit and stare at the baby. Now that I have a baby of my own, I know that parents don't lose the ability to hold an intelligent conversation. We just lose the motivation because we can no longer muster the energy to form complete sentences.

I have been sleep deprived for so long that I can't recall what life was like without a baby—before I required a permanent caffeine drip. I stand in the closet in my underwear and wonder why I'm there. I write notes to myself and then forget where I've put them.

I look at my reflection in the mirror and think, if forty is the new thirty, and fifty is the new forty, then a screaming baby who won't sleep must be the new sixty, because I didn't have these wrinkles and bags under my eyes fifteen months ago.

What I don't understand is how a baby with such a sunny disposition during the day can turn into such a destructive little hurricane at night, letting loose with gale force screams and showers of sobs, then blessing us with two to three hours of eerie calm before he starts all over again. Every morning my husband and I stumble downstairs looking like storm victims. Our eyes are bugged out from being open all night, our hair is dishevelled and our hands shake—even before we chug back our double-long espressos. We collapse into bed well after midnight and half-heartedly talk about having sex. Then Zach wakes up screaming for the third time since we first put him down and we remember how we got into this mess in the first place.

After more than a year of broken sleep we have lost the will to fight. We don't even try to establish proper sleeping habits any-more. These days, it's all about short-term survival. Now when Zach wakes in the middle of the night we just bring him into bed with us. Some nights he sleeps, some nights he stays awake and wants to play, most nights he just squirms and kicks until Andrew and I are left hanging off either side of the bed trying to avoid a foot in the stomach or a left hook to the face. But at least we're all lying down, which is still closer to sleeping than what we've been doing for the past year.

I've read every book there is on getting a baby to sleep and I've tried every method. And every single one of them underestimates Zach's stamina. I know some parents who wholeheartedly endorse the crying-it-out approach. It only takes three days and he'll be sleeping like a baby, they say. Well, they've never seen *my* baby at three in the morning, his face purple, banging his head on the railings of his crib with tears streaming down his face and sobs racking his tiny body.

Maybe he's hungry, maybe he's teething, maybe he needs changing, maybe he's suffering separation anxiety. Or maybe it's me. Maybe I've just done everything wrong. In *Healthy Sleep Habits, Happy Child*, Marc Weissbluth argues that the leading cause of baby sleeping disorders is parents. According to Weissbluth, patting Zach's back, holding him when he cries and rocking him to sleep are all preventing him from learning how to fall asleep on his own.

Well, I don't need Marc Weissbluth to tell me I'm doing everything wrong. I have my mother for that. If parenting is all about instinct, then every instinct I have tells me to run to my baby when he cries out in the middle of the night. When I pick him up from his crib and he wraps his chubby little arms around my neck I know I haven't let him down. So maybe I am doing everything wrong, but it feels so right. After all, he won't be a baby forever— and I can always sleep when I'm dead.

4

A New Dad's Love Affair

A Father's Perspective on New Parenthood

After our son was born, my husband couldn't stop staring at him. He was completely transfixed and desperately in love. "Where did you come from?" he asked in amazement, leaning over the hospital bassinet where Zach was sleeping. Lying in bed recuperating, wondering how nine months of constant care and attention could evaporate in one final push, I yelled out, "Hey, over here! Remember me? I've got six stitches that draw a pretty accurate road map!"

But I couldn't deny my husband his love affair; it had been a long time coming. He was so pleased with himself when it only took a bottle of wine and a shot in the dark to get me pregnant. For nine months he strutted around like a peacock, his virility in full plumage and waving with a pride that said, "That's right, just the one time. You might not want to stand too close, just in case I sneeze...."

So I let him soak up the praise. After all, once conception is complete, the father's role in creating the baby is over. He can't experience the sensation of a baby moving inside him, and while he may sympathize with the symptoms of pregnancy, any pain or discomfort he experiences during those nine months is inflicted by his pregnant partner, not his growing offspring. "You're pretty lucky," I said to my husband one day. "Some women get really hormonal when they're pregnant."

"*Some* women?" he asked, before ducking for cover.

Then the baby arrives and the father can finally take part in the whole parenting game. Except that, for the first few months, the baby is constantly attached to the mother and the studly peacock is demoted to mere orderly—running errands, doing laundry, making dinner; basically, ensuring the household still functions. If he's lucky he'll get a few cuddles in, usually at three or four in the morning when the baby is crying uncontrollably for no reason. His wife has collapsed from exhaustion and he has no idea how to comfort her when she cries out, "I can't do this!" because he has no idea either. He still has to work in the morning—after all, now he has a family to support. The reality of his situation suddenly weighs down heavily and his proud peacock feathers start to droop.

It's not easy being a dad. You don't know anymore than your partner, and you can't blame your mood swings on hormones. Mothers are allowed, even expected, to feel overwhelmed by their new role. Fathers are expected to keep it all together; they are supposed to be the rock, even when they feel themselves rolling off the edge.

Everyone talks about a mother's instinct, but it's actually fathers who operate better with their gut. I am constantly flipping through my baby books to see if I'm doing things right. Andrew uses them as coasters. Once, I pointed out the pile of unread books that I had bought for him, specifically because they were written from a daddy's perspective. I asked him if there was anything about fatherhood he needed help with, or didn't understand. "No," he replied. "But I'm sure if there is, you'll let me know."

After the birth of their first child, a friend of ours asked her husband to read a parenting book during his commute to work. "I don't want to read that stuff in my spare time," he said dismissively. (He later agreed that it was a thoughtless comment, and one that effectively erased any chance of him ever having spare time again.) The point is, men seem to approach parenting books much like they do road maps—they won't consult either until they are hopelessly lost.

While mothers openly fret and worry, fathers can't see what all the fuss is about. After I bought my first pack of baby wipes I found myself suddenly overwhelmed by the distressing realization that I had *no idea* how to take care of a baby. "There's no instructions on these things," I wailed to my husband.

"What do you need instructions for?" he asked. "You wipe their ass and throw it out. Done!"

Fathers are also better equipped to let go. When Zach was learning to take his first steps, it was Andrew who was more willing to let bumps and bruises be part of the learning experience. Babies are designed to bounce, he said. It's not that a father is any less upset when he sees his child lose his balance, it's just that he has more faith they will both survive the fall.

And speaking of fathers, it's not until you become a parent that you finally begin to understand your own. As I watch my husband deal with the emotional and financial pressures of supporting a family, I understand the stress my father must have felt as he searched for a balance between sole breadwinner, authority figure and caring role model. When I listen to Andrew talk about all the things he wants to do with our son—his hopes for Zach's future—I realize how difficult it must have been for my own dad when I made choices that he didn't necessarily agree with, but nonetheless supported. Now I know why his face was so pale during my adolescence.

Not too long ago, I asked my dad when he most enjoyed being a father, expecting him to say, "When you and your sister finally moved out." Instead he replied, "I was happiest in whatever stage I was in. You kids are always so concerned with what comes next. I never looked ahead, I just looked at where I was."

And that's another thing about fathers: they always have something to teach you.

— 5 —

What, Me Worry?
Parental Anxiety

Having a baby is a life-altering experience. It turns a completely normal, rational adult into the type of person who repeatedly holds a mirror under her baby's nose every time he nods off, just to make sure he's still breathing.

So far, the only part of this parenting gig that I seem to have perfected is the worrying. Instead of relaxing into my role as a mother, I have a sequence of different fears that I go through in my head every day; a mental string of prayer beads that I fiddle with constantly. I worry about how life can hurt my little boy, about his health, about whether I'm screwing this job up, and if he'll think I'm boring and like his daddy more. I worry about the friends he'll make, the women who will break his heart. I worry about how we'll manage to send him to university when I'm spending his tuition money at Baby Gap.

Parental anxiety starts the minute you find out you're pregnant. The list of things you shouldn't do and shouldn't eat while pregnant is so long that just about the only "safe" activity is sitting and thinking about all the things you can't do. You become obsessed with the fear that you will somehow harm your baby. I asked my midwife so many neurotic questions during my pregnancy that I'm sure she put a question mark in my file when I mentioned I had never been hospitalized for any condition. And then the baby is born and you realize he was much safer inside of you—when you knew where he was, when he couldn't try to crawl up the stairs as soon as your back was turned, or shove a pen up his nose, or eat dirt.

The newborn stage is the worst. I was terrified that if I held my son too tightly he would break, or that his head would fall off if I forgot to support his neck when I picked him up. I was afraid to give him a bath; if he got wet, I was sure he would slip right through my fingers. I was so paranoid about germs that I would sterilize my breast pump in between breasts because I was worried about cross-contamination. And whenever Zach would pop his soother out of his mouth I would immediately wash it with anti-bacterial soap. It took me about a week to notice that something more than just spit bubbles was blowing out the side of his mouth whenever he used his soother. There was a hole in the nipple. Instead of inhaling germs, my precious baby was sucking back soap.

Fortunately, once I survived those early months I realized Zach wasn't as fragile as I thought. It wasn't long before I felt comfortable throwing him over my shoulder while I vacuumed the house. And now that he's older I spend most of my time trying to convince him that the trash can is not his toy box and the floor is not his dinner tray. These days, if he sucks back antibacterial soap I figure I can skip his bath.

But while I have relaxed a bit about germs, I can't seem to lighten up about much else. My parents don't understand why I'm so anxious all the time. They look around our baby's fortress, previously known as our living room, and shake their heads. "What do you need all that babyproofing stuff for? The kid will stick his finger in an electrical socket, get a shock and not do it again. How do you think they learn?"

Of course, my parents raised children in an era that didn't require car seats, when protecting your house from baby hazards meant using a condom. But the world has changed and the baby-safety industry is making a fortune off the anxiety of new parents—for whom danger lurks behind every unbumpered corner. Even once-innocent childhood pleasures can no longer be enjoyed without fear. I was watching an *Oprah* special once on all the dangerous things babies are exposed to—other than inexperienced parents—and I was horrified to learn that balloons were at the top of the list. Apparently, if a balloon pops and a piece of plastic lodges in the baby's throat he could suffocate. Just the week before, Zach, who was four months old at the time, had his first real belly laugh at the sight of a bright red balloon. Andrew and I spent two solid hours bouncing it off the top of his head. After the *Oprah* show I immediately sent out an all-points bulletin to family members: balloons were to be outlawed from all birthday celebrations. My parents think I'm being ridiculous, but every time I see a balloon I break out into a cold sweat.

Despite parents' best intentions, it is a sad reality that no amount of childproofing can protect babies from parental stupidity. My husband and I have accidentally cut Zach's finger while trying to trim his nails, knocked his head on the door frame while rocking him to sleep and jammed his finger under his dinner tray. And just last week, Zach fell off the bed while my husband was sleeping beside him. Luckily, a pile of books on how to get your baby to sleep through the night broke his fall, so I can finally say they came in handy.

There is no cure for parental anxiety; it's a chronic condition that you learn to live with. You can remember what your life was like before you were a parent, but once you hold your baby, you can no longer imagine what your life would be like without him. You realize it's not the baby who needs protecting. You are now the fragile one, and no safety latch will ever be able to guard your heart from the pain and worry that comes with being a parent.

But with that worry comes the joy of seeing the world through your baby's eyes, a world of magic and discovery, a world without worry. And that's a world I want to live in.

Now if you'll excuse me, I just need to go make sure he's still breathing....

An Odd Threesome

Sex After Baby

Our son was playing in our bedroom the other day and ran off with a pack of condoms that had been sitting on my dresser. I haven't bothered to retrieve them from his toy box. They don't expire for another six years, so I still have time.

The joke that having a baby is the best form of birth control you could ever hope for is so old it's not even a joke anymore. Now it's just an option you tick on your medical history file under contraception: Pill? Diaphragm? Condoms? Children?

Doctors usually recommend waiting six weeks after childbirth before resuming your sex life. We figure we'll just wait until we're ready for another child. It's not that having a baby kills passion in a relationship, it just kills the desire to act on that passion. It's a cruel twist of fate that having a baby has boosted my libido while simultaneously depleting my energy.

When you're only averaging four hours sleep a night, and the rest of your day is spent working—parenting a toddler who has no off switch, cooking three meals a day, eating three meals a day, doing the laundry, cleaning the house and showering—sex almost feels like a flagrant waste of time. "A man has needs," my mother keeps telling me. "You've got to get him back in the saddle."

"I'm trying!" I tell her. But what am I supposed to do if he keeps falling off the horse because he can't keep his eyes open?

Sex changes completely once you become a threesome. In the beginning, you have that awkward fumbling. Your husband doesn't know what to do with your breasts because any kind of stimulation can open the dairy bar and it just doesn't feel right to be playing with your baby's lunch. And then there's the fact that a woman's body does change after childbirth. It's no longer just a vehicle for her partner's pleasure, it's also a delivery truck—and one in bad need of a lube job before it heads back out on the road.

When I confessed to my midwife that I was a bit anxious about resuming a sex life post-baby, she suggested using lubricant jelly for the first few times, just in case it was uncomfortable. I shouldn't have worried. The sex wasn't half as uncomfortable as going into the drugstore, picking up the first tube of lubricant I could find, blurting out, "Thirteen dollars?! For *lubricant*?!" at the cash register, and then making the ten customers behind me wait while I ran back to find a cheaper brand.

Even though your sex life does change after you have a baby, it can still be exciting.

My husband and I will still rip each other's clothes off in the heat of the moment, it's just that, these days, it's usually because we only have half an hour before the baby wakes up. And we never skip the foreplay, although it no longer involves kisses and caresses. Now we just kick each other in bed and say, "It's your turn to go get him." "No, I went last night, you go."

The best part about sex now that I am a mother is that it takes much less to get me in the mood. Forget wining and dining. If my husband wants to get lucky, all he needs to do is start mopping the floor or pick up the vacuum. And if I ever see him on his hands

and knees scrubbing the toilet, I think I'll just light myself a ciga-
rette and call it a night.

You can still have a healthy sex life and a baby—after all, there
are plenty of couples who have more than one child. But it is quite
possible that the kind of pre-baby sex we once enjoyed is now per-
manently a thing of the past—we'll just never have that kind of
energy or spare time again. Whenever I start to get depressed
about this new reality, I remind myself that relationships are a
constant ebb and flow. Andrew and I are still deeply attracted to
each other, and one day Zach *will* sleep through the night, or leave
for university. Until then, we'll just have to find a way of having
sex that doesn't require moving—or waking up.

—7—

The Mini Food Critic
Starting Your Baby on Solids

I was so excited when I first started Zach on solids. I thought of all the quality family time we would spend around the dinner table. My husband and I would interact with Zach and provide stimulating conversation while he would marvel at all the new tastes and textures we had so thoughtfully prepared for him.

Well, the stimulating conversation begins and ends with, "DO NOT shove that up your nose!" and I'm too busy interacting with the mop to spend any quality time with Zach. He doesn't seem to mind. He's having too much fun tossing his dinner on the floor, throwing it at the walls and shoving it in the little crevices of his high chair—putting it everywhere but in his mouth.

There are few things I have found more confusing about motherhood than starting solids.

When do you start? What do you introduce first? What are the possible allergens? Just how much protein, iron, vitamin C and calcium is there in one forkful of scrambled egg, a bite of toast and one banana that hasn't really been eaten but rather smeared over the baby's face? And what about the time Zach ate a picture of an apple from one of his board books? Was that one serving of fruit, or one serving of fibre?

Because I was living in the U.K. when I got pregnant, I have a lot of British books on pregnancy and parenting. These often have a different perspective than the books written in Canada. Apparently, British babies can start solids at four months, but Canadian babies should be exclusively breast-fed until at least six months. Since Zach spent eight months in utero in the U.K., I took a chance he had enough British in him to handle some rice cereal. At four-and-a-half months he weighed close to twenty pounds and nursed almost every half-hour. My breasts were begging for some time off.

I probably should have waited. While I could now extend the time between nursing sessions, I suddenly found myself doing double duty in the kitchen—pureeing batches of sweet potatoes, spoon-feeding cereal and constantly hosing down my son who absolutely refused to wear a bib. I obsessed over whether he was getting a balanced diet and all the right nutrients.

Introducing a baby to solid food, I've discovered, is no piece of cake, especially once that baby is old enough to form opinions on what you're feeding him. Andrew and I are adventurous and enthusiastic eaters, so cooking meals for a picky baby can be frustrating; it's like trying to feed foie gras to someone who would rather eat processed lunch meat from a tin can. I'll present Zach with some new appetizing food, and usually he'll just clamp his mouth shut and turn away. Really, why would he eat a perfectly cooked strip of marinated chicken when he can have a dried up piece of tofu wiener that he stored under the sofa last week? Other days, he'll just wail, which at least gives me the opportunity to shove something in.

For a baby who regularly munches on the insoles of his father's shoes, Zach is quite the food critic. With one fell swoop of his chubby little arm he will knock everything off his tray, as if to say, "That's what I think about that meal!" And there is nothing more irritating than to watch him pick up a piece of food—food that I've spent half the day preparing just for him—and casually dump it on the floor, watching as it falls to see what kind of mess it will make. I can see his little mind working as he peers over the side of the high chair: "Hmmm, will spaghetti splatter or just sit there in a lump like the cauliflower she tried to pass off on me yesterday?" It has occurred to me that I am paying good money to cover my floor in organic food.

Lately Zach has started covering his eyes with his hands before opening his mouth, as if he can't bear to see what I'm feeding him. Frankly, I find it insulting. I try to mix vegetables and meat with pasta or mashed potatoes but he's incredibly fussy about taste and texture. He will spit out an entire mouthful of food, find the offending piece, pick it out, and then abandon the entire meal in disgust.

Our dinner table has become a messy battleground—every night I soldier on and continue throwing food at Zach (and ducking its return) until he surrenders and accepts something. I can hear the panel of parenting experts in my head, judging my perform-ance, and telling me that I should only offer my child what I have made for that meal. No substitutions, they say. Hunger will soon teach him he needs to eat. But I don't want to send my baby to bed with an empty stomach. I am aware that he could be manipulating me. I suppose if he can understand, "Would you like a cookie?" he can figure out how to convince me to give him a cookie instead of mushy peas. But at least he's eating something—which means I can rule out hunger as one of the hundred other things that might be waking him up at three in the morning.

I sincerely hope that Zach will become more adventurous as he gets older, because there are very few restaurants that serve miniature yogourts and animal crackers. But for the moment, my little food critic seems well nourished and content with his diet. And if he could talk I'm sure he would question my preference for squid and escargot. "Really, Mommy," he would say. "There is no accounting for taste."

—8—

Say What?

A Baby's First Words

I was so excited when my son first started to speak. "Zach said fish!" I bragged to my mother. "Don't push him too hard," she warned me, before pulling out her old joke: "I spent the first few years of your life encouraging you to talk and walk—and the rest of your childhood trying to get you to shut up and sit down."

I'm sure the time will come when my son's incessant call of "Mummy!"—in the little New Zealand accent that he inherited from his father—will start to grate on my nerves. But for now, each time I hear it my hearts melts. Like most babies, Zach's first coherent babble was "da-da," and whenever he wanted to be picked up or was upset he would cry out "da-da-deeeeeeee." If he wanted me, he would just point and grunt. It took nineteen months of prodding before I started getting the recognition I deserved.

The development of speech is such an amazing milestone. For the first year of parenthood, it's hard to see past the exhaustion, the steady stream of dirty diapers and the endless breast-feeding sessions. "Savour the early days of your baby's life," my parents told me. "They pass by so quickly."

"Oh really?" I snapped. "Then why am I still sitting here nursing him?"

Then, one day, Zach's gurgles and coos turned into real words and I realized that those early days were indeed over. He is no longer a passive infant; he is growing into his own little person— independent of me—and it thrills me and breaks my heart all at the same time. Before he could speak I only suspected he might prefer Daddy's company to mine. There's no denying it now as he pushes away from me and stands at the front door crying, "Where's Daddy?"

But I've come to love the fact he is learning to express himself by talking, not just screaming. As he soaks up every new word, I can share in his sense of wonder at this exciting world around him. And the months of miscommunication no longer matter when he utters the one phrase I waited a year and half to hear: "Tired. Night-night." I could nearly weep.

I watch him place words and concepts together like pieces of a puzzle. He will point at a Starbucks cup and say, "coffee," a fountain and say, "water," the TV and say, "where's Dora?" His mind is like a vacuum on maximum suction, it takes in everything and the house echoes with all the new sounds he has picked up. He yells out, "Oh no, Zach!" when he spills something. He shakes his head from side to side and says, "Oh, gawd," when I change a particularly stinky diaper. And one night when I walked past his crib I heard him call out, "Train! Choo choo!" in his sleep.

But even though Zach has begun to talk, we don't always speak the same language. Half the time I have no idea what my son is saying. He will shake with excitement as he tries to tell me something, but after I venture four or five guesses he just throws his hands in the air in exasperation and waddles away as if to say, "Oh, never mind!"

Luckily he doesn't let the frustration get to him. Now that he has found his voice, he is determined never to lose it. He used to wake up screaming in the middle of the night for no apparent reason, now it's to draw us into the room so he can talk. He can be sobbing hysterically, but as soon as the exhausted shadow of what used to be a normally functioning adult appears in his doorway, he will turn, smile and say, "Hi!" in his most charming baby voice. Then he'll start chatting away, as if the last four hours of sleep were just an inconvenient break in the flow of his conversation.

I'll gather him up from the crib and he'll snuggle into my neck giggling, "It's a mummy!" It's a pretty accurate description; after months and months of broken sleep, I feel like I have been dead for a thousand years.

But I still love to hear that word.

9

The First Time

Surviving the First Moments of Parenthood

We recently went to a first birthday party for a friend's daughter. My friend said she wept when she woke up that day, completely overwhelmed by the passing of that first significant year. On my son's first birthday I cried too. I baked three *Finding Nemo* birthday cakes and not one of them turned out. My parents had flown to Vancouver for the occasion, we had gathered around the table with party favours and the video camera and Zach had fallen asleep, entirely unaware of his momentous achievement in turning one.

It occurred to me then that maybe parents spend too much time recording the events of a baby's first year. Every moment of a baby's life is a first during that year: his first smile, the first time he rolls over, his first tooth, his first temper tantrum.

Rather than track every first moment of the baby's life, I thought, maybe we should track the first moments for parents. The first time you took your baby to the doctor for an immunization and didn't cry when they stuck the needle into his soft baby flesh. The first time you didn't gasp when he pulled himself up on the coffee table. The first time he threw up on your sofa and you didn't care. The first time you left him with a babysitter. The first time you discovered it was possible to have a conversation with a stranger with your breast hanging out. The first time you felt like you knew what you were doing (I'm still waiting for that one).

I remember the first time that I was really scared as a parent. It was when Zach had a severe allergic reaction to salmon. Andrew had been calmly feeding him a mashed up salmon patty when red blotches suddenly spread all over Zach's body with the speed of a forest fire in the heat of summer. He started crying and pulling at his skin while Andrew and I ran around in a panic. I called the maternity care hotline and told a nurse what had happened. She told me to hang up right away and call 911. The paramedics arrived at our house within seven minutes and gave Zach a shot of epinephrine to stop the reaction.

A number of things race through a parent's mind when their child is in danger, and like the fight-or-flight response, you choose to escape the thought of what your life would be like without your baby and you focus on the ridiculous. There I was holding my wheezing son, trying to quell the pounding fear that had replaced my heartbeat, and all I could think to myself was, "God, I hope the paramedics don't put that grubby medical box on my white couch!"

Thankfully, Zach recovered. Within the hour he was flirting with the nurses and doctors in the emergency room at the hospital, happily playing with a tongue depressor. Andrew and I, on the other hand, now suffer from regular palpitations.

I realized then, for the first time, that being a parent meant I had better get used to living with my heart in my throat and my stomach in knots. What if he falls out of a tree and breaks his arm in a few years time? What if a bully chases him around the kindergarten schoolyard with a salmon sandwich, or he gets hit by a car riding his bike, or falls in with the wrong crowd in high school? How do you deal with illnesses like the measles—or adolescence? How do you keep your heart from breaking under the pressure of everything your child needs to be protected from, when you can't promise you'll always be able to protect him?

You can't. Parenthood is a tightrope. You walk it gingerly, because there is always a pit of worry and fear beneath you. There is no end to the tightrope; you can't stop being a parent, and you will never find yourself walking above safe ground. But if you remain centred, you can gather the hugs, and the kisses, the laughter and the love—all the rewards of parenthood—with each baby step you take.

So, to all the parents who have walked that first-year tightrope and survived, throw yourselves a party! Bring out the cake and the champagne! Celebrate and have a drink—because now you are the parent of a toddler, and trust me, you're going to need one.

Part 11
When Toddlers Happen
to Good People

10

Baby Is a Four-Letter Word

Temper Tantrums

Motherhood definitely has its moments, like when my son toddles towards me, wraps his arms around my neck and giggles, "Mommy!" My heart bursts with the pure pleasure of being his first love—being his mother.

And then there are the days when my little cherub rears his head back and smashes me in the face because he doesn't want to be held, even though two minutes ago he was tugging on my leg to be picked up. The days when he decides he doesn't want to play with his Bob the Builder truck and throws it on the floor in a rage—and my foot conveniently breaks its fall. The days when changing a diaper turns into a dirty wrestling match and I wonder why the mothers on the Pampers commercials never have to pin down a squirming baby and field kicks to their jaw. The days when I try to put him in the car seat and his arms and legs spread stiff and straight. He arches his back and howls his refusal for everyone in a ten-kilometre radius to hear. It's like trying to put a cat in a carrier box so you can take it to the vet: there's just no way the job is getting done without some scratching and biting.

Some days, baby is a four-letter word.

I'm not sure where my son learned to scream, to throw tantrums and to lash out. He can't be mimicking how *we* behave. When I pass my husband a glass of milk he doesn't throw his head back, chuck stuff on the floor and cry uncontrollably. (He saves that kind of behaviour for the privacy of our bedroom, when I tell him I'm too tired for sex.) And it's not like my son has fallen in with a delinquent gang of toddlers who have influenced his behaviour.

Babies, it seems, don't need to be taught how to break the sound barrier with cries of protest, or how to spin around the house in a fury like a pint-sized tornado, leaving a trail of destruction and spewed toys in their wake. *They just know.*

Don't get me wrong, Zach isn't a demon all of the time. For the most part he is a curious, happy, engaging, active, good-natured baby with a smile and laugh so infectious that I often feel I could have three more just like him. Really, it's only when he's tired, or bored, or hungry, or wet, or dirty, or teething or not feeling well, or when I do something obvious to provoke him—like offer an apple instead of a banana—that the monster within breaks loose. Without warning he'll hurl himself on the floor with a deafening wail, his face will flame red and his arms and legs will swing wildly as if there's some crazy puppeteer pulling his strings.

I've learned to ignore him when he gets like this—at home. But in public it's difficult to deny he's my son, especially when he keeps pointing at me in hysterics, sobbing "Moooooommeeeeee!" So I gather him up from the playground or the grocery store and try to ignore all of the other mothers—who are doing their best to avoid eye contact anyway.

I realize that babies go through phases, that some stages of development are more trying than others, that my son is—God help me—normal. But it still doesn't make the irrational outbursts, the unpredictable mood swings and the teeth marks any easier to handle.

"It will pass," my mother keeps reassuring me, and I know she's right. I'm sure that Zach will eventually grow out of temper tantrums. I've already noticed that after months of diving for the floor, Zach now puts his hands out first, looks to see where his head is going to land and then decides whether or not it's worth it. And I'm sure that his burgeoning language skills are helping too. He's been expressing himself more clearly lately by screaming out new words like "NO!" and "MY truck!" so I feel like we're communicating. It shouldn't be too long before I can sit him down and ask, "Now Zach, tell me, what were you feeling when you threw your truck at Mommy's head?"

Yes, I'm sure that once this phase is over, motherhood will be much easier....

Flying with a Toddler?

Pass the Parachute

Welcome aboard, ladies and gentlemen. For those parents flying with infants under six months, please insert breast or bottle at regular intervals to ensure a smooth ride. An air hostess will be by shortly after takeoff to assist you by entertaining your baby while you relax and enjoy a beverage.

For parents flying with babies a year or over, please remain at the back of the plane and fasten your seatbelts tightly. You're in for one bumpy ride. Please secure the bag of toys you brought to entertain your toddler in the overhead compartment to ensure the safety of the other passengers. Airborne plastic trucks are considered to be hazardous. Please do not allow your baby to repeatedly hit the call button; it is not to be used as in-flight entertainment. Please be advised that the emergency exits do not operate once we are in the air, no matter how loud your toddler is screaming, or how many other passengers he may be terrorizing. An air hostess will be by shortly after landing to assist you off the plane. Enjoy your flight!

Flying with a toddler is a completely different experience than flying with an infant. Infants are easily contained. Toddlers are like miniature volcanoes: they constantly erupt, they spew noxious substances everywhere and you definitely don't want to be sitting next to one.

When Zach was fifteen months old I decided to fly back to Ontario with him on my own. We were going to visit my parents while Andrew stayed in Vancouver to catch up on work and some much needed sleep. We had taken Zach on a plane twice before his first birthday, and both times were incident-free. How hard could it be on my own? If only someone had told me that, when you fly on your own, you leave behind the only other person you can blame for your baby's behaviour.

I gave Zach a dose of Gravol just before takeoff. All the friends I knew who had flown with a toddler swore that some mild drugging would help him sleep through the flight. I learned two very important lessons during that flight: 1) Parenting advice is selective. There will always be one baby who is the exception to the rule—which is why the warning label on the back of the Gravol bottle reads, "Caution, may cause drowsiness OR excitability." Giving Zach Gravol was like spiking a triple espresso with speed. And, 2) When flying with a toddler, it's the parent who should be medicated.

Trying to hold an active toddler on your lap for four hours is like trying to rope a bull calf, and just as dangerous. As Zach struggled to get free he bit, scratched, pummelled and head butted me so many times I seriously considered getting a restraining order for the return flight. When he wasn't screaming, he kicked the seat in front of me, played peek-a-boo with the guy behind me and pulled the hair of the lady beside me. I let him loose down the aisle in front of me hoping it would calm him down, but he was so happy to be walking that he smacked each armrest, resting elbow and napping head in excitement as he went by. I even tried bribing him with crackers to keep him quiet, but the lady sitting across from us was getting tired of fishing them out of her coffee cup.

Normally when I fly, I never go to the bathroom without first grabbing all my belongings. I have this paranoid fear that some-one might rifle through my purse, pocket some cash or worse, steal my identity. On this particular flight, however, I was fairly certain that nobody on that plane wanted to be me, so I eventually rushed to the bathroom, leaving everything I owned behind so I could try to contain my little menace in private. But nothing worked; my attempts to control my son were about as effective as sticking my hand in a blender to slow it down. In desperation I adopted the parenting crash position: I kept my head down, avoided all eye contact and repeated over and over, "This too shall pass...."

And then, miraculously, the plane landed and the flight was over. And just like the storm clouds that lift to reveal a shining sun, Zach greeted my parents at the Toronto airport with smiles and giggles. We strapped him in the car seat and he slept soundly for the two-hour drive back to their house.

My husband thinks I'm exaggerating. He can't believe his adorable son was that difficult to fly with. But then, he thought morning sickness was all in my head, so what the hell does he know? He wants to take Zach to New Zealand this year to show him where his daddy grew up. I say Zach can wait until he's a bit older to see New Zealand, like when he's eighteen.

And maybe by then, we'll be allowed back on an airplane.

12

Life in the Trenches

How Do You Discipline a Two-Foot Dictator?

My opinion is that the future good or bad conduct of a child depends on its mother.

—Letizia Ramolino Buonaparte (Napoleon's mother)

My in-laws dropped in unexpectedly the other day. From New Zealand. I'm all for last-minute guests. I always have the ingredients on hand for a quick cocktail and we have a good pizza delivery place on speed dial. But if you want to visit a clean house, with a composed hostess and a well-behaved baby, I need at least a month's notice. Hell, who am I kidding? If you want to visit a clean house, a composed hostess and a well-behaved baby, you don't need to give me a month's notice, you need to visit someone else.

When I complained to my parents that Zach was throwing regular temper tantrums and had started biting me they both said the same thing, "You need to step on that young man before he gets out of hand." Which just goes to show that my parents are completely out of touch with parenting today—Zach is already way out of hand.

I try, I really do. I set boundaries; I have perfected my "don't mess with me" voice; I practice divert-and-distract techniques; and I tolerate mini meltdowns—usually mine. But sometimes I wonder if my parents are right, if I am too soft. But how do you discipline a toddler? He is no longer an infant, but he is not yet a child. He needs guidance, not just nurturing. But how do you reason with someone who believes that by smearing his lunch on the wall he's feeding his shadow? We're in a state of discipline limbo.

My parents don't have much time for the new methods of behaviour modification touted in my parenting books. "If Zach bites you, bite him back," they both insist. But despite their assertion that it will work, I refuse to bite Zach back, partly because I don't think he would understand what I was trying to teach him by retaliating with the exact behaviour I'm trying to stop. But mostly, he doesn't need any pointers on how to improve his technique. Not to mention that the whole thing seems kind of barbaric—like when my grandmother would wash my mouth out with soap if I ever uttered a bad word in her presence, which never really seemed fair since I learned most of the words from her.

With Zach, I went for the more modern approach and gave him a "timeout" in his playpen—from which he immediately catapulted himself out. Landing on his head did not improve his behaviour. Friends of mine swear by the "naughty mat"—introduced to North America by the U.K.'s celebrity Supernanny, Jo Frost. Apparently, forcing a toddler to sit still in one place for even a minute is like a form of torture and will definitely have him re-evaluating his behaviour. Well, if I knew how to get my son to sit still in one place for one minute or longer, I wouldn't need a naughty mat in the first place.

At first, I just didn't believe that a toddler could be purposely naughty. I tried to explain to my parents that Zach didn't draw on my white dining room chair with a pen because he knew he shouldn't. All he saw was a perfect canvas and a great opportunity. It was my fault for thinking I could have a baby living in the same house as furniture that can't be dry cleaned.

Of course, I was forced to re-evaluate my position a few months later. Now Zach will grab the pen, wait for me to notice, raise his eyebrows and flash me his most charming smile—and then scribble all over the chair before making a run for it. Does anyone have the Supernanny's number?

"He needs a spanking," my parents keep telling me. "You would get a spanking once a month at his age," my mom said. "It was like a woman's period. You would start acting up—and you would always get worse by the third week. Then I would give you a spanking and all would be right again for another month."

"I am not going to spank my son!" I exclaimed. "I just don't think it's the right way to instill good behaviour."

"You're going to lose all control over that boy if you're not careful," she warned me.

"Really Mom, it's not like he's out robbing liquor stores. He just threw my cell phone in the toilet."

"Fine. Do it your way, then," she sighed in a tone that implied my way would have me visiting Zach through plexiglass in twenty years' time.

"You know," a friend of mine said the other day over coffee. "You might want to reconsider your stance on spanking. Because let me tell you, there have been times when I have been so frustrated that I feel like throwing my kids out the window . . . not that I ever would of course," she quickly qualified as she drained her cup. "But a spanking doesn't seem like such a bad compromise after that."

There are definitely days when my patience and endurance are challenged; when my failure to get my son to eat his meals, go to sleep or stop throwing his toys on the floor has me wondering if an obedient, well-behaved child without authoritarian rule is simply incompatible—like wanting a retirement plan *and* a decent shoe collection. And then I think maybe it has nothing to do with discipline techniques. Maybe I'm just ignoring the opportunities to instill proper behaviour. I still remember an episode when Zach was around sixteen months old. We were walking past a toy store and he started pointing frantically at the display window, yelling out "TRAIN!" I was so impressed that he could pick out a train among all the other toys in the window, that I rushed into the store with my wallet open, ready to reward my son for displaying such genius qualities. The only thing that stopped me from buying it for Zach—who was by this time hysterically yelling out "TRAIN!! TRAIN!!!"—was the forty-dollar price tag.

Perhaps sensing Mommy's limited budget he quickly turned towards a basket of plastic trucks for ten dollars and yelled out, "TRUCK, TRUCK!!" Looking back, I realize it was at this point that I should have walked out—empty-handed—to show Zach that crying and pointing is not the way to ask for something. But that's how I got the wedding ring I wanted, so who am I to say anything?

My mother-in-law warned me that if I let Zach win one battle, I might as well surrender to a life ruled by my baby. Well, I lose battles on a daily basis, but why should raising a baby be a war? Sure, some days I feel like I'm living in the trenches—my clothes are covered in food and juice stains, and I have to duck flying building blocks that Zach launches like makeshift ammunition— but I don't consider him my enemy, although some days I do feel he may be the death of me. We're both on the same side, and when he grabs hold of me as if I'm the only person who will ever be able to make him happy, I know I'm winning more times than I lose.

I remember when I first brought Zach home from the hospital. I was completely overwhelmed by my new responsibility. I knew when to feed him, and when to change him, but after that I was at a loss. I asked my midwife what else I was supposed to do, how I was supposed to be a mother. "All you have to do is love him," she said. "You'll figure out the rest along the way."

And if there are things I can't figure out, I'm sure Zach's correction officer will be able to help me.

13

Can I Get You the Cheque?
Eating Out with a Toddler

Mothers are not normal people. Normal people do not spend nine months in training just so they can push a bowling ball through the eye of a needle. Normal people do not take a twenty-month-old to a restaurant and expect to have a happy family outing.

When you have a baby, your family and friends all warn you that your life is about to change dramatically. But of course you don't believe them. Nothing needs to change, you think. Life will continue as normal. Which is why you continue to do normal adult things with your baby—like eating out—just to prove them wrong.

But of course they're right. Life is no longer normal. Normal people don't need to book a table for six just so they can accommodate two adults, a toddler, a stroller, a diaper bag, a high chair, a fleet of plastic trucks and an emergency supply of cookies and applesauce.

Normal people do not take turns chugging coffee and shovelling in food while the other desperately tries to avert a toddler meltdown by playing peek-a-boo behind a menu, making happy faces out of sugar packets and turning cutlery into dancing puppet shows. Normal people don't rush out of a restaurant, holding a two-foot firecracker at arms length that suddenly set off when faced with the indignity of having to sit in a high chair.

Normal people would say, "Why don't you get a babysitter?" But mothers know that babysitters cost ten dollars an hour— which is money that could be better spent on dessert, or a second martini. And if you're eating out with a toddler you're definitely going to need a few.

Parents are well aware that they are the least popular patrons in a restaurant. When waiters spy us walking in holding our thirty-pound live wire, our faces shining with an apologetic smile, we know they're going to draw straws to see who gets stuck with us. As we walk to our table, other customers without children treat us like the smelly kid on the school bus. They avert their eyes, shift their bags to take up extra space, hold their breath and pray, "Please don't sit next to me."

"Don't worry," I want to tell them. "You'll hear him from across the room anyway."

Despite our unpopularity, my husband and I will continue to pay good money to pick food off the floor and out of our hair, even though we can do it at home for free. We do it for the same reason we call our car "the sexy four-door hatch-back": because no matter how thrilled we are to be parents, neither one of is ready to admit we're actually driving a station wagon. We will continue to deny that our lives have changed—even though we now make dinner reservations for four-forty-five p.m. and we study a kids' menu instead of a wine list.

I know I'm not just entertaining a party of one here. I know there are plenty of other mothers sitting at the same table as me— trying to hang on to a life that no longer exists. I've seen them in parks and coffee shops across the city; they will continue talking to a friend, calmly polishing off a cup of coffee and a muffin, while their child is throwing a fit beside them in a stroller. It's a small act of defiance and it declares, "I was a woman before I was a mother, and I am going to sit here for five more minutes and try to remember how that woman used to live.... Okay, four more minutes ... Okay, maybe just two. Fine! Let's just get out of here, but when we get home I am going to read five pages of a magazine, undisturbed. Okay, four. Okay, maybe just two...."

I was at Old Navy last week, desperately searching for an outfit that would repel stains and disguise baby fat. But instead of trying clothes on, I found myself on the floor with my butt in the air, trying to coax my son out from under a shelf of long-sleeved cotton shirts. As I dragged him towards me, he kicked his arms and legs in protest and medium and large tops started flying like we were at a Boxing Day sale. Zach finally emerged from the shelf with a price tag dangling from his mouth and I started to laugh. "This is not how normal people shop," I thought. Then I reminded myself, "I'm not a normal person. I'm a mother." I pulled out my cell phone and called my husband. "Hi honey," I said. "Why don't we go out for dinner tonight?"

Call me crazy (or call me Mommy, I answer to both), but I actually look forward to dining out as a family. Eating in public with a combustible twenty-month-old may be as relaxing as a root canal, but hell, even a trip to the dentist gets you out of the house. And I'm sure there will come a day when my son's attention span will last longer than it takes the waiter to ask, "What can I get you?"

And as I pull out my credit card to pay the bill, I think to myself:

Brunch for two adults: $30.

One bite taken from a child's order of waffles: $8 (plus one extra month of sit-ups because I end up finishing it).

Cost of covering the damage caused by my toddler after he sneaks a sip of my double espresso: an additional 35 percent gratuity.

Eating a meal I don't have to prepare, and using a bathroom I don't have to clean: Priceless.

14

Thank Heaven for Little Boys

Nature or Nurture?

There are a few things I know now that I am a mother. I know the difference between a dump truck and a front-end loader; I know who Bob the Builder is; I know which baby clothes will best hide the dirt; I know there is a show called *Mighty Machines*. I have even watched it.

One of the biggest adjustments for me as a mother hasn't been learning to live with a baby, it's been learning to live with a *boy*. I never had a brother. I grew up surrounded by women—my mother, my sister and a dozen female cousins. My mother said my father was the only male we needed in the house, so even all our pets were female. In fact, my son is the first male born into the extended Sager family in thirty years. I was about as prepared for a son as the *Titanic* was for the iceberg.

I was talking to a friend of mine about life with a baby boy. While she commiserated as a fellow mother, she admitted she just couldn't personally relate to the chaos I described. She has a daughter, born with an apparent behavioural defect that causes her to sleep twelve hours straight every night, prevents her from throwing tantrums and has left her saddled with a compliant and agreeable nature. Two weeks ago this friend had her second child—a healthy robust son. She's still recovering from her eighteen-hour, ten-pound introduction to chaos.

"They just never stop," complained another friend, whose son is almost two. "It's like overdrive is the only gear they have." And she's right. I spend most of my days chasing after Zach—who can move faster than an Olympic sprinter—and most of my nights desperately searching for a button that will turn him off, or at least mute the screaming.

Is it nature or nurture? Are little boys really hyper, aggressive and combustible, or do parents just encourage it? Sure I dress my son in blue, but I'm certainly not training him to operate on warp speed. I never taught him how to chuck his toys so they bounce off various parts of my body, or how to throw his head back so it connects perfectly with my nose. When we visit the playground I don't encourage him to ignore the swings and roll around in the mud instead. And not once have I ever suggested screeching was the best way to get my attention, or that four hours was considered an acceptable night's sleep. No, it's definitely nature. You can give birth to a boy, but you can't create one. Why would you do that to yourself?

Even my parents admit they don't know how to help me; their experience raising two manageable girls has given them nothing to draw on when dealing with their grandson. The last time my parents came to visit my mother declared she would be able to train Zach to sleep through the night. He broke her at about four a.m. "I feel so sorry for you," she said—right before she and my father checked into a hotel.

The truth is, boys and girls are different—from the way they develop to the way that they play. Parents of a baby girl don't need to worry about jumping back when changing a diaper. Parents of a baby boy, on the other hand, know that as soon as you free willy it will start spraying like an uncontrollable garden hose. Anatomical differences aside, I do try to be careful not to treat my son any differently than I would a daughter. I have invested in all the non-gender-specific toys on the market, and it still hasn't made any difference in the way Zach plays; if it doesn't look like a truck, sound like a truck and crash like a truck, then it's not a truck. Zach has a basketful of cuddly stuffed animals gathering dust, and if he ever picked up a doll it would only be to see what kind of noise it would make when he chucked it down the stairs. I even enrolled him in a ballet class. Of course, there was that little incident just last week. Zach—who is the only male in the class—was uncharacteristically sitting by the sidelines. I tried to encourage him to join the others and was horrified to hear myself say, "Come on, Zach, are you going to let a bunch of *girls* show you up?"

Okay, so maybe nurture does have a little something to do with it, but in spite of the male and female characteristics we parents may inadvertently push onto our children, they already know who they are. This past Christmas while we were visiting my parents, my mother was giving Zach a bath. He was standing up in the tub and holding his penis, staring at it inquisitively. "What are you doing, Zach?" my mother asked. "Penis," he finally said, repeating the word his daddy had taught him. Then he sighed, "Happy."

My son has introduced me to a whole new world, a world completely alien to the neat, contained and obedient one I grew up in. A world where every day is an adventure—a high-energy, high-impact, high-volume adventure. He runs first, ducks later. Jumps high and lands hard. He hugs like a bear and bites and punches like a miniature Mike Tyson. He screams with laughter, cries in floods and kisses with a big juicy smack. He runs on full steam, while most days I run on empty. You can't deny genetics.

Male stereotypes were born from generations of exhausted mothers yelling, "Get your finger out of your nose and climb down off the dinner table before you crack your skull open!" He is a boy—a messy, loud, volatile, incredible, lovable boy.

I'm learning to love this new world, despite the nervous twitch I have acquired. A baby boy may be difficult now, but I'm very familiar with a girl's world and have no desire to live through another female adolescence. Besides, for the first few years at least, a mommy is the most beautiful woman in the world to her son.

I can live with that.

15

Sit, Baby! Sit!

The Parallels of Parenting— Raising a Child and Training a Dog

Parenting has many odd parallels; you could compare it to, say, trying to have sex in the shower. As soon as you feel like you've got a good grip on the situation you start to relax. Before you know it, you've slipped and landed on your butt with a thud, and you're wondering why you ever thought this was going to be so easy.

And you could say that parenting is an awful lot like owning a dog. If you are a good master you will be rewarded with a lifetime of sloppy kisses and unconditional love. If you're lucky, you might even get your slippers and newspaper delivered every morning.

If you think about it, a toddler is really just a puppy with opposable thumbs. My son leaps over to me, tail wagging, tongue flapping, ready to play all the time. He follows me around the house, drooling and licking at my heels, begging me to pick him up or give him a cookie. He has chewed on my shoes, my furniture and enough books to poo out an entire children's library.

He will perform tricks for the amusement of a crowd. "Watch this!" I said to my parents when he first became mobile. "If I put a toy in front of him he'll crawl right to it!" I even have one of those toddler leashes to prevent him from darting away from me in public for an impromptu game of hide and seek. And as he barrels ahead like a St. Bernard in heat, I think how perfectly it illustrates my walk through parenthood so far—my son is in the lead, and I am running behind, wheezing, desperately trying to catch up.

"Anyone who wants a child should have a dog first," a friend told me. "Everything I know about raising a baby, I learned first with my dog: patience, discipline, toilet training. Having a dog lets you figure out your parenting style ahead of time. Are you going to be the authoritarian owner who raps your dog on the nose every time he does something wrong, the permissive owner who spoils your dog with treats or the authoritative owner who is firm but flexible?"

Maybe she's right. After all, her son will sit when told to, eat when given food, come when called and sleep when shown his bed. I wonder if my breed of puppy is untrainable, or if maybe I'm just barking up the wrong parenting techniques.

Harold Hansen, author of *The Dog Trainer's Guide to Parenting*, believes that anyone can apply the basics of dog training to child rearing. According to Hansen, children often misbehave because they are confused by a parent's command. He suggests that before speaking, parents should decide whether "No!" means never, not now or stop. But who has time to decide? When my son stuffs something up his nose, or unplugs my computer right before I've hit the "save" button, "No!" is the quickest way to touch on all three. I understand what he's getting at though. If you hear something too many times, you learn to block it out. Like when my husband opens the Visa bill and exclaims, "You bought another pair of shoes?" My conditioned response is, "Would you like another cup of coffee?"

One thing is for certain, parents and dog owners both have the same insecurities and anxieties about raising their brood. A quick scan of titles like *Mother Knows Best: The Natural Way to Train Your Dog*, *How to Talk to Your Dog* and *The Perfect Puppy: How to Raise a Well-Behaved Dog* reveal we are all just looking for some guidance—some way to housebreak our little animals without breaking their spirits.

As I was thumbing my way through *The Secrets to Fixing Any Dog Problem*, it occurred to me that I could have written this book. I could use everything I know about parenting a toddler to teach people about dogs.

Q: "What's the secret to housebreaking your dog in a hurry?"
A: Send him to Grandma's house for the weekend.

Q: "How do you praise your dog so your praise has meaning?"
A: Say, "Good boy, now here's a cookie."

Q: "What's the most important thing you need to know before you hire a dog trainer?"
A: Will your husband find her attractive?

And finally:
Q: "What is the terrible truth about training the pit bull?"
A: They will bite the hand that feeds them.

Part III

Does My Bum Look Big in This? Fitting into Motherhood

My Mother Never Told Me There Would Be Days Like This

Adjusting to My New Full-time Job

I had no idea how motherhood was going to change my life. My mother never told me. When I asked her what childbirth was like, she said, "Oh, it's nothing more than you can bear." Which really didn't help prepare me for what felt like the lower half of my body exploding.

And she certainly never prepared me for the lifestyle change of the stay-at-home mom. It wasn't until I had a baby of my own that I finally understood why she wandered around the house muttering, "I might as well have a vacuum cleaner strapped to my back...."

When my husband and I were newlyweds I loved playing house. Three years, one baby, and a million loads of laundry later, this game is starting to feel more like a chore. I think of all the things that mothers have to juggle in a day and I wonder why we continue to debate whether women can have it all. Who wants to have it all? Where would you keep it, and who would have to clean it?

I am still surprised by the sheer amount of domestic drudgery that is involved in raising a family. The speed at which the piles of dirty dishes, the loads of laundry and the toys reproduce in our house has me terrified that if I close my eyes I'll get buried alive. There are days when I feel like I'm stuck in a time warp. I wonder how a post-grad degree managed to dump me at the kitchen sink with a baby crawling between my ankles. I'm the modern day Stepford wife—but without the lobotomy. Or Nicole Kidman's cool, retro wardrobe.

"But you work from home," my mom reminded me. "You write a column! You're like the Carrie Bradshaw of motherhood!" Right, but without the regular sex life. Or Sarah Jessica Parker's wardrobe. Damn, I really need to go shopping.

Maybe my mother never told me how hard staying at home was going to be because she never really found it all that difficult. The feminist movement may have been sweeping the country in the seventies, but it barely brushed past our small Ontario town. My mother was never expected to have a career; in our house, the roles of breadwinner and caregiver were clearly defined and respected.

My mother never questioned the fact that women bear the children—and most of the domestic burden. She instilled in me a sense of servitude that was passed down to her from her mother. And, like the extra four inches around my hips that I also inherited from her, I just can't shake it. We were visiting my parents in Ontario this past summer and it had been a particularly rough morning with Zach. I had just managed to put him down for a nap when my father and husband pulled into the driveway fresh off the golf course. "Your husband is home," my mother said. "You had better make him some lunch."

"Unless he broke his arm on the eighteenth hole he can make his own lunch," I replied as I went to take a bite out of my tuna sandwich. And then she gave me *the look*—the one I've been practising in the mirror my whole life but have yet to master; the one that made me put down my sandwich and make my husband lunch, because no matter how liberated I like to believe I am, you can't fight breeding.

Maybe my mother never told me there would be days I would question myself, days when I would struggle with my decision to stay at home, because she never felt like she was supposed to be doing something else. There was nothing else she wanted to do. And maybe she never worried about trying to have it all, because to her, she already did.

But this is the twenty-first century! I'm supposed to be conquering the world of publishing, or running my own magazine. Or doing something that requires a Chanel power suit. I'm supposed to feel guilty because my son is in daycare. I'm supposed to be wondering whether he's stimulated properly and worrying about how our relationship will be affected because I'm never home. Instead, I'm feeling guilty because I have to put Zach in front of the TV so I can write my column or do the laundry before it crawls down to the washing machine on its own. I wonder whether I'm stimulating him properly and I worry about how our relationship will be affected because I'm always home.

I do have ambitions, although I'm too tired at the moment to remember what they are. I still want to conquer the publishing world, but right now I'm busy rewriting all of Zach's bedtime stories. Seriously, how many times should a person be expected to read *Goodnight Moon*?

It's not that I resent staying at home. I resent being the only one who ever scrubs the toilet, but I don't resent staying home to raise my son. I just never knew it was going to be such a difficult job until I was actually hired. My old colleagues—the ones who chose a different career path—pat me on the head and tell me what important work I'm doing, but when I try to talk about how overwhelmed and exhausted I am, their eyes glaze over with boredom. I can see them thinking, "How hard can it be? Staying at home with a baby is not exactly rocket science."

"Why don't you nap when the baby naps?" they suggest breezily, as if all the work and anxiety in my in-tray will simply stop piling up while I take a break for an hour.

When I was first recruited for this job, no one told me my boss would be ridiculously temperamental and prone to irrational outbursts. He rarely allows me a full lunch hour and I only get a coffee break if I push the stroller to Starbucks. I work for free, and while hugs and kisses are wonderful bonuses, they cannot always be guaranteed. I am subjected to daily peer reviews at the park or the supermarket as I navigate tantrums and submit to his authority out of pure desperation. I am at his beck and call, and when I tuck him in at night I find myself looking forward to another day of exactly the same thing. I must be crazy, or in love.

Being a mother has taught me more than just how to change a diaper in the dark. It has taught me how to redefine the way I view success. I may not be enjoying the high-powered career that I once thought I would have, but I'm well aware there are women who ache for my job as mommy. And if I screw this up, there's a lot more at stake than a promotion. There are days when I long for that feeling of accomplishment I had in the "real" world, the world that rewarded my efforts with an actual paycheque. But while I may not contribute as much financially as my husband, a family is a long-term investment—and I made a pretty significant deposit into our joint account when I gave birth.

My boss can be a tyrant, but he needs me. Despite the bad days and the chaos, I'm happy with my role as a stay-at-home mommy. The work may be tough, but at least I can do it in my pyjamas.

17

Can I Get This in Another Size?
Body Image After Childbirth

A woman's body after pregnancy and childbirth is like a cashmere sweater washed in the heavy-duty cycle. It comes out intact but it just doesn't fit like it used to. It's stretched around the middle and sags in places where it used to hug. You can still wear it—you just don't like the look of it on you anymore.

When I was pregnant my body felt like a science experiment out of control. A bit of chemistry in the bedroom was the catalyst for a bizarre transformation that continued even after childbirth, morphing my body into something completely unrecognizable. My once firm belly has been replaced by an expanse of Jell-O. The voluptuous breasts I had during pregnancy and while nursing now look pale and exhausted, as if they could use a good two weeks of recuperation on a beach in the Caribbean.

My shoulders and hips are wider, my thighs are thicker, I no longer have extra pregnancy fat to fluff out my cellulite, and I can store my sunglasses in the hole that used to be my belly button. I don't know whether it was giving birth to my son or to my uterus, but I now have one section of hair at the back of my head that is curly while the rest is straight.

Women's magazines, doctors, pregnancy books and people who haven't had children all claim that doing Kegel exercises will tighten your pelvic floor muscles and help stop incontinence, especially after childbirth. Well, they work about as well as a strainer would if you needed a bailing bucket. I did Kegels before I got pregnant and all during my pregnancy, and it didn't make any difference. For ten months after Zach was born I had to put on a pair of rubber boots before I sneezed.

Evolution has seen to it that women create new fat cells in their last trimester of pregnancy. The theory is, we can use these cells to store extra energy as a way of protecting ourselves and our babies from starvation. Apparently, evolution hasn't heard of twenty-four-hour take out. We don't need to store extra energy; we can just order it when we need it. Baby fat is stubborn. Like reality TV, it just won't go away. I can now sympathize with a friend of mine who was once asked when her baby was due. "Nine months ago!" she cried out.

I did consider going on a no-carb diet to lose the weight, but then I realized that a life without cake is not a life I want to live. Instead, I'm on the toddler diet. I mostly eat pieces of soggy bagel, leftover spaghetti, discarded chunks of apple and bits of animal crackers. I may not be losing any weight, but I'm moving all the time and I've got the biceps of a body builder from lifting my thirty-pound bundle of joy twenty times a day.

My exercise regime consists of daily lunges with the vacuum cleaner, squatting to fold laundry, pushing the stroller and running up and down the stairs after Zach. I don't bother trying to do sit-ups anymore because I know if I lie down on the exercise mat I'll just fall asleep.

Looking at my body now I think it's not so much accepting my new shape that's so difficult. It's saying goodbye to my body before baby that's the hard part. The body that was younger, and firmer, and could eat fast food and still fit into my favourite pair of jeans. A body that could stay up past ten.

Then I remind myself—I have created life, I am woman! My child-bearing hips may not have made labour any easier but now they provide a nice little shelf to prop up my son—who cares if I need to walk through the door sideways to clear the frame? And Zach gets a kick out of squeezing the rolls of fat on my stomach and back, so I'm saving money on educational toys.

And what's the point in trying to regain my old shape? If we want another baby I'll just have to do it all over again, and I hate to do a job more than once. Six months into a second pregnancy, my belly will look firm again—massive and rounded, but firm. Besides, all those women who haven't yet challenged their bodies with pregnancy and childbirth—the ones who can actually fit into size one at the Gap—will be in big trouble if they ever find them-selves in the middle of a famine. But thanks to evolution, I will be happily living off my baby fat.

Now, could you pass that last piece of cake please?

18

According to the Experts
A Whole New Chapter of Neuroses

When I was pregnant with Zach I was diagnosed with "Listeria hysteria" by my doctor after a severe panic attack was brought on by a slice of unpasteurized cheese.

"Oh my God," I remember saying. "Is it serious?"

"It can be," she replied. "The only cure is to stop reading the Internet and pregnancy books."

Too late. I had already contracted a hopeless addiction. I signed up for a pregnancy calendar so I could track my baby's development from the moment of conception—and then spent the rest of my pregnancy in a perpetual state of worry. During the week my baby was busy growing eyebrows I freaked out because I had walked through an airport security gate. "What if I hurt the baby?" I thought to myself. "What if my baby only grows one eyebrow because I wanted to go on holiday? I'm a terrible mother already!" It was a long nine months.

And then my bundle of joy finally arrived and opened a whole new chapter of neuroses. I became a book parent, and a library of expert opinions moved into our house, occupying the chairs where, in previous generations, mothers and grandmothers used to sit. But the more familiar I became with my adopted family of parenting professionals, the more confused I became. As I tried to sift through all their conflicting advice I felt like I was being cornered at a family reunion. There's the uncle who warns, "Spare the rod, spoil the child!" while his wife yells out, "Listen to your child, take your cues from him!" There's the sister who suggests co-sleeping, and the sister-in-law who advocates crying it out.

There's the grandfather who grumbles, "If you pick that boy up too much, you're going to spoil him." The grandmother who says, "If you don't give that boy enough attention you'll end up with crazy uncle Ted." The in-laws who ask incredibly, "You weaned him already? I hope the baby is only eating organic homemade food. Are you feeding him too much? He looks too heavy." The parents who say, "When are you going to get that kid off the boob? There's nothing wrong with bottled baby food—you grew up on it. Are you feeding him enough? He looks too thin."

And of course, there are the cousins who don't have any children of their own, but have taken some university courses on early childhood development and, "If you don't mind me saying so, maybe you should try it this way?"

Like a teenager, I rebelled, "If you experts are all so smart, why can't any of you get my baby to sleep through the night?"

You have no choice but to listen to your family's advice. Either through birth or marriage, relatives are the prize you find in a box of Cracker Jack—free with purchase. Parenting experts on the other hand, need no such pre-existing relationship to tell you what they think, and they certainly don't need to wait for an invitation to Sunday dinner before invading your home. Even if you manage to avoid reading any parenting books, as soon as you turn on the TV, experts from shows like the *Supernanny*, *Dr. Phil* and *Nanny 911* fill your living room with dire pronouncements about how parents are doing it all wrong. You're sitting in front of the TV with your finger wavering over the off button on the remote control, trying to remember when it was you asked them in, but afraid to turf them out—just in case you are doing it all wrong.

One night, as I was getting dinner ready, my husband was watching TV in the next room when I heard a commercial advertising a *Dr. Phil* special on parenting. As I ducked my head in and out of the refrigerator, grabbing food for our meal, all I heard was, "Are you raising a serial killer?" and "Does your child watch too much TV?" I rushed into the living room and started recounting the amount of TV Zach had watched that day. "Oh no!" I cried out to my husband, "Zach watched *Dora the Explorer* today, *Bob the Builder*, some of the *Mole Sisters* and maybe ten minutes of a *Baby Einstein* video. What have I done?"

The fear that I had just tucked in Ted Bundy kept me up until ten p.m. when Dr. Phil's show came on. I discovered that TV watching has absolutely nothing to do with raising a serial killer, but juxtaposing the two is a clever way to get parents to forgo a few precious hours of sleep to watch a parenting show. (Although most serial killers do share one common experience—a screwed-up relationship with their mother—so the pressure's not off.) I also discovered that compared to the people Dr. Phil was dealing with I'm doing a pretty amazing job. I decided to start hanging out with families who were more dysfunctional than mine so I could give myself a confidence boost.

But at least the experts only imply you're doing things wrong. With real family, there's no doubt. After a day of meltdowns, tantrums and bite marks, I asked my mother if I was screwing up as a parent. "Oh honey," she said and gave me a reassuring hug. "Not if you stop now."

And then I met Ann Douglas, the author of *The Mother of All Toddler Books* and the woman who single-handedly restored my faith in experts. We chatted over coffee about the highs and lows of motherhood while my son demonstrated the latter, shrieking with impatience the whole time. But Ann never flinched. I made a mental note: read "Master the Art of Selective Ignoring" (page 185).

What I liked about Ann was the fact that she's an expert who doesn't claim to be an expert. She's a mother of four who still struggles to find a balance between family, work and other obligations. She is against following parenting fads over gut instinct; she rules with kindness and respect and dismisses "one-size-fits-all parenting solutions," claiming they fit most parents and kids as well as one-size-fits-all jeans.

I asked her why she thought mothers today put so much pressure on themselves to do everything perfectly. "I think it's because our kids matters so much to us, and because so much of our identity as women is tied up in the motherhood role," she replied. "We may not care if we have dust bunnies breeding under the couch or if we're the worst cooks in the world, but most of us would be totally devastated if we turned out to be 'bad mothers.'" She leaned in closer as if revealing a secret. "While it may not be possible to be a perfect parent," she confided. "It's quite possible to be a good parent. That frees us and our kids from the tyranny of trying to be perfect."

Just when I was ready to divorce my experts for irreconcilable differences Ann came along and said something that made perfect sense. "We're the only true experts when it comes to our own kids." We spend too much time second-guessing ourselves, she told me. "Sometimes our society whitewashes the truth about new motherhood, something that can leave new mothers feeling isolated, incompetent and terribly alone. We assume everyone else is doing a better job than we are, when that's simply not the case." Aha! I thought. I knew it! She must have watched the *Dr. Phil* show, too.

Finally, an expert who admits to chaos, who parents with her heart and who doesn't aim to be a perfect parent, but a good parent. Ann is the black sheep of my family of experts. Too bad she isn't real family—then I could ask her to baby-sit.

19

Do You Come Here Often?

Feeling Isolated as a Stay-at-Home Mom

> Stay-at-home mommy seeks same for play dates, emotional support and conversation without rhymes, sing-song voices or commands to "get your head out of the toilet!" Please, no decaf drinkers or Atkins dieters. If you don't eat cake, we probably won't be able to be friends. Call anytime.

When my husband and I left London for Vancouver, I was completely unprepared for how lonely parenthood can be. Our families were on opposite sides of the globe with one set in New Zealand and the other in Ontario. Most of our friends were still in London, the rest were scattered around the world. The few people I did know in Vancouver were either working or busy with their own families. Pretty soon my childless friends had stopped calling: new moms are scary with their horror stories of labour, sleep deprivation and engorged breasts. It was just as well—I didn't have the energy to answer when they asked, "What do you do at home all day?"

My life may have been full with the joys and stresses of motherhood, but I had never felt more alone. Everyone already had their own little clique and I was the new kid in school, wandering the halls aimlessly, a lonely misfit just looking for someone to have lunch with. In one transatlantic trip to a new city and to motherhood I lost two pieces of luggage—my old body and an active social life. I'm certainly never flying that airline again.

Andrew had set up a wine-importing business from home in a bid to balance work and family, so he became my social network. But after a few months he told me I wasn't allowed to talk to him during the day anymore. Apparently he couldn't get anything done because I kept interrupting him to ask if he was ready for a coffee break. So I was forced out of the house in search of someone else to talk to.

It's an awkward activity looking for new friends when you're a stay-at-home mommy—it's like dating but without the sex (okay, maybe it's more like marriage). Except you no longer hang out at singles joints chugging back shots of tequila, you hang out at Gymboree classes and coffee shops, chugging back shots of espresso. And instead of being impressed by someone with a fancy Italian sports car, you now chase down the mommy with the expensive imported stroller to ask her where she bought it.

Your pick-up lines change from, "Do you come here often?" to "Didn't we meet in the Baby Bubbles swim class?" You still exchange numbers and wait by the phone, but you no longer worry that someone didn't call back because of something you did. Now you worry a mommy didn't call back because your baby hit hers over the head with a sand shovel at the park.

But some things are the same. Some dates never go any further than the first cup of coffee. A few months ago I met some new mommies at a lunch thrown by a mutual friend. As we chatted, one of the women asked if we had seen the *Oprah* show on mothers who drink. "They were interviewing this woman who took a Thermos of vodka and lemonade to the park. Can you imagine?"

"Well, that's just wrong," I said. "If you're going to take a Thermos to the park, it should be Baileys and coffee." There was some nervous, polite laughter, but I never did hear from any of them again. Maybe they lost my number?

And we still get involved in relationships of convenience only to break them off a few weeks later. You can bond with a mom over sleep deprivation, colic and sore nipples. But if her baby starts to sleep through the night, the colic disappears and her nipples clear up, you may find you no longer have anything to talk about. It's time to move on. You might bump into each other at the grocery store one day and exchange a few pleasantries, but you both know the magic is gone.

Advances can still be rebuffed. Committing to a baby is enough of a job, making new friends can sometimes feel like just one more chore. I tried striking up a conversation once with a mommy at my son's ballet class after Zach had accidentally twirled into her daughter, knocking her flat on her tutu. She just nodded politely, gathered up her daughter and returned to her friends, leaving me wondering if I had forgotten to brush my teeth again before leaving the house. Or was Tuesday the day I usually forgot to apply deodorant? Who can keep it straight? It's a big enough achievement if I can remember to put on underwear every morning.

And, like dating, we still size each other up based on appearances. Whenever I'm scoping out the park for new mom friends, I always do a quick head to toe scan. If a mom's stomach looks flat and toned I usually give her a wide berth—I'm looking for friends I will have something in common with. I also tend to avoid women who look more exhausted and frazzled than me—I'm looking for friends who can babysit. Which, come to think of it, could be the reason why mothers tend to avoid me.

And, just like dating, if you stick at it long enough, you'll eventually get lucky. You will meet mommies you connect with—even beyond motherhood. Because, just like life, motherhood is a wonderful trip—but no one wants to ride it alone.

20

The Two of Me
Before- and After-Baby Personalities

I have a split personality. There is the Me Before Baby and the Me After Baby. The Me Before Baby has been relegated to the far corners of my mind, but she still fights for her old dominance. She bats away at the cobwebs, and yells out over the background hum of children's songs and grocery list recitations: "Remember when you said your child would never act that way; you would never do that as a parent; that raising a baby couldn't possibly be that hard; and you weren't going to turn into your mother? Remember?!"

I have tried to merge my two personalities—if only to stop the voices in my head—but they can't be reconciled. The Me After Baby is slowly taking over. The Me Before Baby doesn't live here anymore, she tells me. There is no room in here for a woman who thought she knew everything, who was used to eight hours sleep every night, who had little responsibility, who expected this job to be easy, who never had to worry she was doing it all wrong.

When I'm out shopping with Zach and he howls at the injustice of being wheeled around a store that sells nothing of interest to a toddler, I can hear the voice of Me Before Baby whispering, "I would never allow my child to act like that in public. I would take him straight home, that would teach him to behave!" But the Me After Baby isn't listening anymore, because I really don't get out that often—and I'm holding the last top in my size. And besides, if leaving a store as soon as a tantrum starts hasn't taught my husband how to behave while out shopping, why should it work with my son?

It's ironic. Before you become a parent you seem to know so much about parenting. Once you finally have a child of your own, however, you realize you know absolutely nothing. When I first got pregnant I told my mother that my husband and I didn't believe having a baby would change our lives. "There's no need to let a baby consume us," I said with the cocky assurance of someone who had no idea what she was talking about. "The baby should be able to conform to our lives." She raised an eyebrow, and in a voice laden with accumulated years of parenting wisdom, chuckled, "Good luck with that."

A few months ago a friend of mine—nine months pregnant with her first child—spoke in that same cocky tone when I complained about my son's nocturnal habits. "There's no reason he can't sleep through the night," she told me. "You must be doing something wrong. When our baby is born he'll be on a sleeping schedule right from the very beginning." I was too tired to laugh, so I just said, "Good luck with that."

Everything changes once you have a baby, especially your conceptions about parenthood. When I used to imagine myself as a mother I was usually framed in a Baby Gap commercial with an adorable, giggly baby planted stylishly on my hip. I would be standing in a field of dandelions and smiling at the camera with the wind blowing through my hair and ruffling my maternal yet still sexy sundress. But the Me After Baby knows that motherhood cannot be captured in a Baby Gap commercial, and that babies are not accessories. Trust me, a screaming toddler does not complement any outfit.

Even though I was adamant it wouldn't happen, my son's complete dependence and utter vulnerability, his continuing development and emerging personality have wholly consumed me. And if I had been able to make Zach conform to my life he would already be toddling down to the kitchen at eight in the morning and making Mommy an espresso. Instead, it's me who has adapted as I drag myself out of bed at four a.m. to rock him back to sleep.

It's a humbling experience being a parent. I know there will be more moments ahead when my son will behave in ways I swore no child of mine ever would, when I will make mistakes and compromises I said I never would, when I will start to say things like, "Because I said so!" Parenthood, I have discovered, is a whole other dimension. Like the alien species on the Star Trek *Enterprise*, the Me After Baby towers over the cocky, self-assured Me Before Baby and says, "Resistance is futile. You will be assimilated." There's no denying it: I am turning into my mother. But I'm also discovering that's not such a bad thing—although I'll never let her know that.

I will miss the Me Before Baby. She seemed to know so much about being a parent, and had so much more free time. But she is just a distant memory—sort of like my sex life. Although I do still catch glimpses of her every now and then in other Before Baby women, like the last time Andrew and I flew from Toronto to Vancouver with Zach. Boarding the plane lugging two armloads of supplies—essential when travelling with a two-year-old to any destination further than the corner store—we wistfully recalled the days when carry-on luggage meant a credit card and a clean change of underwear. We were busy stowing our things, securing Zach's car seat and praying that his low-lying grumbling wouldn't escalate into a full-blown tantrum when the lady in the aisle seat across from us—a few years older than me and perfectly manicured and composed in a way that only a person who has yet to know the joys of parenthood can pull off—leaned over and asked me, "Now, will your son fuss the entire way to Vancouver? What should I expect? Will he sleep? What do you intend to do about it because I'm on my way to Australia and I honestly can't handle too much noise right now."

And suddenly, there in Aisle K, with a diaper in one hand and a bottle of Extra Strength Tylenol in the other, I realized that Me Before Baby and Me After Baby no longer had anything in common. I was embarrassed and absolutely mortified that this woman, who would be able to eat a hot meal, watch a movie and read a trashy magazine all before we landed, would actually voice *out loud* the kinds of thoughts that once ran through my mind before I knew the trauma of flying with a toddler. "SLEEP?!" I wanted to scream. "Do you think I would look like this if I could get my son to sleep?!"

I also had no desire to admit to this lady that our trip out to Toronto had consisted of three hours and fifty-five minutes of Zach screaming, and one rather large domestic meltdown between Andrew and myself. I had little faith that our sole plan of attack for this leg—strapping Zach into his car seat and plying him with an arsenal of books, snacks, sippy cups, *Baby Einstein* DVDs and matchbox cars—would do much to ensure a smooth flight. So, instead I smiled sweetly and said, "Australia? Really? I used to live in Australia. Beautiful country. Shame about all those poisonous spiders though, really does put a damper on things. Luckily there's only a few that can kill you, and only one that will hurt you so bad you'll wish it killed you. If you run into any problems, try to catch the spider after it bites you so the doctors will know what kind of medicine to give you. Hope you have a great trip."

I turned towards Zach and happily pulled out a book while she slumped back into her seat, her composure slightly ruffled. She never even flinched when Zach started screaming. I guess she had other stuff on her mind.

Yes, it's the Me-After-Baby personality that has taken over; she is who I am now. She knows nothing at all about being a parent, but she's learning.

21

Things I Don't Understand About Motherhood

(How Much Time Do You Have?)

Parenthood is a steep learning curve. There aren't any crash courses you can take beforehand, so new parents are forced to learn on the job. After almost two years in this position, I feel I have amassed a certain amount of knowledge about being a mother. But as I sit here trying to figure out exactly when I lost my living room and gained a playground, I can't help but ponder some of parenthood's little idiosyncrasies—the ones that aren't explained in the parenting books.

For example, how come the Bugaboo Frog Stroller—one of the most high-tech, versatile, functional and achingly trendy strollers on the market—costs $1,200 but doesn't come with a spot to stash your coffee cup? The Bugaboo boasts it is "redefining mobility," but no matter how high-tech it is, it still hasn't redefined the reason we pack our babies into a stroller in the first place: so mommy can walk to Starbucks. It has, however, redefined what parents now consider a reasonable amount to spend on a stroller.

What does the tag "not intended for sleepwear" mean? Shouldn't the people who design baby outfits take into account the fact that babies will often fall asleep unexpectedly? I remember panicking when Zach was only a few months old and had fallen asleep in an outfit "not intended for sleepwear."

"I have to get this off of him!" I shouted to Andrew. "He's not supposed to fall asleep in it!" Of course, once I managed to undress him, the problem was solved. He was no longer sleeping, but he was a little pissed off. These days I don't care what Zach falls asleep in, I just want him to fall asleep.

Why didn't *he* come with a tag attached that reads, "not designed for sleeping"?

Why is it that all these sleep experts guarantee they can get your baby to sleep through the night if you just follow their advice, but not one of them ever publishes their home phone number so you can call them at three in the morning to ask for your money back?

How is it that I'm still standing after the kind of intense sleep deprivation that could fell an army of soldiers? Apparently, lack of sleep is responsible for some of the world's biggest disasters, like the Exxon oil spill. And my kitchen.

When did I start sounding like my mother? I find myself saying things like, "What did I just say?" after yet another parental request goes ignored. At the moment, my son's vocabulary allows him complicated sentences like, "My truck" and "I want," but I stand there, staring at him with my hands on my hips, trying to practise my stern face, as if I honestly expect him to answer, "Well, Mommy, as I recall, you asked me nicely not to place your shoes in the dishwasher because the dishwasher is for dishes. It's not a shoe rack. And then you said something about me driving you crazy. Does that mean we're going somewhere?! Can we go to the park?!"

What the hell is a Boohbah?

Why is it that toy manufacturers can make a toy safe and easy enough for an eighteen-month-old to use, but the parent needs an engineering degree and a tool box to release the bloody thing from all its packaging?

If scientists can figure out how to get baby toothpaste to taste like bubblegum why can't they figure out how to get fat-free chocolate to taste like chocolate? The American Academy of Pediatrics recommends flossing a toddler's teeth once two teeth start to touch, but why don't they offer any instructions on how to do it without losing a finger?

Why am I always running around but still unable to lose the rest of my baby fat? And why have I never been able to regain the self-confidence and extreme pride in my body that I felt when I gave birth to my son? I didn't obsess about my cellulite and whether my butt looked big when I was squatting on the delivery room table, so why do I care now?

How can the best thing that ever happened to me strip away my self-esteem in an instant, reduce me to tears and then, with one adoring smile or fierce hug, instantly make me feel like a hero?

Why is it that as soon as you get a handle on one stage of your baby's development, he will move on to another? And how can parenthood be exhilarating and heartbreaking, all at the same time?

Maybe part of the joy of parenthood is not having all the answers; maybe it's about learning and discovering together with your child. After all, it's the only game where you are actually allowed to make the rules up as you go along. Maybe there are just things we aren't meant to understand—like how to fold a fitted sheet, and why a bikini costs twice as much as a one-piece, even though there is half the material? And why do parents love their children—desperately and passionately, celebrating their every accomplishment, encouraging each tentative step towards independence—all the while knowing we are teaching them how to leave us?

I guess there's just no explaining it.

Time Off For Good Behaviour
Play school

There are brief periods of calm in the life of the stay at home mommy, moments when we can sit in the eye of the storm, savour the warm comfort of an uninterrupted triple latte, and peacefully observe the chaos swirling around us without being drawn in. Like naptime. Or the thirty minutes it takes to play a *Baby Einstein* video. But the most delicious refuge I have discovered so far—this side of a tub of Häagen-Dazs chocolate-chip cookie dough—is Play School. For two hours a day, three times a week—and without mommy—my son gets to socialize with other two-year-olds, paint, sing, play on the jungle gym outside, read stories, engage in stimulating activities and run around a confined space that is not my living room. Like my ice cream, Play School feels like a guilty pleasure; I'm a stay-at-home mom, and here I am enrolling my child in what could be considered a glorified daycare (despite being advertised as a "preparation for preschool" program). But everyone has their crutch. My son only needs a two-minute catnap to recharge his batteries—if we could sell his internal wiring to Duracell, we would make a fortune. Mommy, on the other hand, needs a little longer. After all, even criminals get time off for good behaviour.

As much as I desired an outlet to preserve my sanity, it wasn't easy letting go. I was a panicked mess as we made our way towards the Play School building on Zach's first day. How could I leave my precious baby with total strangers, I asked myself. What if Zach took off as soon as one of the teachers turned her head; it happened to me on a daily basis. What if one of the other toddlers gave Zach a bite of their salmon sandwich? Would the teachers know how to call 911? What if he started to pick up bad habits that I couldn't fix, or his personality started to change? What if he hated it? Or worse, what if he had more fun with them than he did with me? Maybe I was rushing things, I thought when we reached the door. It was just too soon to risk being replaced.

I was ready to turn around and go home when the doors opened and Zach caught sight of the bounty inside. "Trucks!" he yelped, and in an instant he was gone. Three other two-year-olds followed closely behind, leaving a group of bewildered mothers—who had prepared themselves for a long, drawn out goodbye—standing around, cursing our children's short memories and ingratitude. I felt like yelling out, "Hey kid, remember me? I nearly died in labour, come back here and give me a hug! Show me some tears!" At this rate, once he turns three and starts preschool, all he'll need from me will be five dollars for lunch and a map to get home.

Through the door I watched my little boy run up to a group of other children, his face beaming with his wraparound smile. He cried out, "Hi guys! I'm Zach," as if to say, "The party starts now!" The crowd parted obligingly, drew him in and the play resumed. I was overcome with pride at my son's easy adjustment, but had to catch my breath as this new step towards independence rapped at my heart like a drinking glass hitting the counter, causing a tiny, almost invisible crack to etch its way down the side. I know the glass can still hold water—for years even—but it will always be just one more knock away from shattering completely.

It was odd. Once I had the free time I had so desperately coveted, I wasn't quite sure what to do with myself. I was an act without a sidekick. I reasoned that with six hours every week, all to myself, I could easily work on my writing, or catch up on the housework. But then again, that would screw up my regular schedule of writing when I'm supposed to be doing housework, and doing housework when I'm supposed to be writing.

Luckily, mothers are masters of adaptation, and I quickly learned that there was an amazing amount of things you could accomplish in one day with two hours to yourself. One morning I treated myself to a manicure and a massage, and then relaxed in the sunshine with a coffee on the patio outside my local Starbucks. A woman I had met in Gymboree class pulled up to the coffee shop in her minivan and rushed out looking haggard and exhausted, her infant and toddler crying in the backseat. "Oh, thank God I ran into you," she said. "Can you just watch the kids while I run in and get a coffee? It's been a hellish morning."

"Sure," I nodded. "No problem."

"Wait a minute," she stopped herself, looking around. "Where's Zach?"

"He's at Play School," I replied, smiling. "I have to pick him up in twenty minutes, I just had a massage and a manicure," I told her, showing off my nails.

"Wow," she said, a touch of envy in her voice. "You just look so relaxed. Like you don't even have kids."

"Really?" I asked, flattered. "Because that was the look I was going for."

As much as I enjoy my mini-break from motherhood, I actually look forward to the end of each class, when Zach runs out of the door and into my arms, giggling, "Mommy! Mommy!

Mommy!" When I ask the teacher how he was, she laughs and says, "Great, but we still can't get him to touch any fruits or vegetables at snack time." Excellent, I think, it's not just me who can't crack this particular food aversion. "Well," I say, "hopefully it's just a phase."

"You know," the teacher said to me last week, pulling me aside. "Zach just loves it here." My stomach dropped. Just as I'd feared, he was having more fun with them. "But five minutes before every class ends, he runs for the door to wait for you." I smiled, and swallowed back a mixture of happiness that my son does miss me, and guilt that I am enjoying our time apart.

But mothers must learn to adapt, I remind myself. So the next time I drop Zach off at Play School, I think I'll go for a pedicure instead.

Living With Labels

Mommy Types

When I was a teenager, I thought there could be no experience more painful than high school. Of course, I was younger then, what did I know? I had yet to be subjected to childbirth without an epidural—or an entire season of *The Simple Life*. Yes, life can be full of pain.

I got a chance to relive those self-conscious days of bad acne and dubious wardrobe choices when I caught that ultimate teenage flick, *The Breakfast Club*, on television the other day. Five high school students spend a day together in detention and realize that the silly labels that divide them do not actually define them. That, as one character put it, people see you as they want to see you—in the most simple of terms, in the most convenient of definitions—when in fact, each one of them is a brain, an athlete, a basket case, a princess and a criminal. Fast-forward fifteen years or so, substitute detention for a full morning of Gymboree before you've had a cup of coffee (a similar punishment) and you have *The Mommy Club*. Because discovering what type of mother you are really is a rite of passage much like surviving high school—and just as awkward.

As a mother, it's easy to get lumped into set categories, each with its own defining characteristics: the working mom, who is never there; the stay-at-home mom, who is always there; the slacker mom, who is only half there; the hyper-competitive mom, who is everywhere better than you; the stylish mom, who looks better everywhere than you do; the anxious and paranoid mom, who worries here, there and everywhere; and the hippie mom, who is only there if organic, homemade food is being served. But instead of whispering with a friend behind a locker door over a person in another clique, mothers roll their eyes at one another over the swing set while observing the group by the jungle gym. Luckily, what you wear is no longer the source of anxiety it was in high school (especially since Lululemon has made it possible for just about everyone's ass to look good in a pair of sweatpants). Now it's what our children wear, the stroller we buy, the parenting style we favour and our child's behavioural tendencies that determine our pecking order in the playground.

I wonder why we have such a need to label mothers, but as a friend pointed out, "If you don't label something, you'll never get help for it."

I'm quite aware of how my often frazzled and exhausted demeanour is used to identify what type of mother I am. I remember a conversation I had once with a fellow mom, whose views on sleeping I found to be quite militant. The world came to a standstill between twelve and one-thirty for naptime, all excursions were planned around this small window and the schedule was never revised or interrupted. Bedtime was strictly observed at seven every night, no exceptions. Granted she had more energy than any other mother I have met so far, and her child, of course, slept dutifully for twelve straight hours. She visibly blanched when I laughed about my son's erratic sleeping habits, and I knew I had been immediately placed in the slacker category. "I put my son on a strict schedule," she said. "Sleep is just too important to me." I rushed home to Andrew, "I know why we can't get Zach to sleep through the night!" I exclaimed. "Why?" he asked, pausing for a moment before shooting back his double espresso. "Because, sleep is just not that important to us!"

Despite feeling like I may not fit neatly into just one specific category, I am guilty of classifying mothers in the same way—like the paranoid mother I met at the park a few weeks ago. A friend and I had to stifle a laugh as we watched her nervously eye a panel van that had parked outside the playground. The owner of the van was long gone; we had watched him walk towards the public gym beside the park, a set of boxing gloves dangling over his shoulder. "I think it's strange that someone parked a van outside a playground, don't you?" she asked us. The anxiety eventually became too much and she pulled out her cell phone and called the local police department. "I'd like to report a suspicious vehicle," she said. "It's a white van parked outside a playground . . . No, there's nobody inside . . . Well, don't you think that's strange? . . . Would you like the license number? . . . Can I speak to your supervisor?"

The funny thing is that while every mommy "type" has a specific set of characteristics, none of the traits are exclusive and binding. And when it comes to tough issues like breast-feeding, discipline approaches, returning to work and vaccinations, it would appear that all mothers have experienced, in varying degrees, a bit of righteousness, anxiety and confusion. Motherhood really is as angst-ridden as those self-conscious days of high school when we struggled to figure out who we were. And just like in high school, we are all wandering down the same halls together. Labels may separate us, but we all share certain qualities.

Above all, the one thing we share in common is the desire to love, nurture and support a child, who will, by most estimates, move out in eighteen to twenty years, taking most of our energy, sanity, groceries and savings with him. So whether you are a working mom, a stay-at-home mom, a slacker mom, a hyper-competitive mom, a stylish mom, an anxious and paranoid mom, or a hippie mom, one thing is for certain. We're all nuts.

Does that answer your question? Sincerely yours, The Mommy Club.

— 24 —

Let's Be Honest
The Truth About Motherhood

One day shortly after my son turned one, a friend and I were having lunch. I asked her if she found it monotonous being a stay-at-home mom. "I know it's exhausting, and we're always busy looking after them," I said. "But don't you sometimes, find it just a bit ... *boring?*"

She looked at me strangely and replied, "No. No I don't," and then quickly excused herself, leaving me to stare at my half-eaten sandwich, wondering if there was something wrong with me. Was I the only mother who felt this way? Did other mothers crawl into the nursery in the middle of the night to calm their screaming baby, feeling frazzled and emotionally empty, and think, I just want someone else to come and do this for me? Surely I can't be the only one who dreads going to a drop-in tot gym on a rainy day because, while being in a room full of toddlers racing around in a fleet of Little Tykes cars may be an enjoyable way for my son to spend a morning, for me, it's a Tylenol commercial in production. Or does admitting out loud to things like boredom, frustration and anger only lead to more guilt about not being a good enough mother?

The hell with it, I thought. There's an empty bag of Oreo cookies hidden in the trash bin that I demolished in one sitting. I have enough to feel guilty about. Let's be honest with each other: Motherhood is messy—let's chuck the guilt! In an attempt to reassure other mothers who have hidden the fact that they feel slightly ridiculous waving a parachute up and down, trying to mimic lyrics to a children's song that everyone else seems to know, I have compiled the following truths about motherhood. At least, these are the ones that I have discovered so far.

No matter how many frequent flyer points you have accumulated, you will never get upgraded on an airplane if you fly with a toddler. You'll be lucky if they even let you on the plane.

Stains will come out of a baby's ten-dollar outfit, but not the forty-dollar one.

Despite the number of books you read on parenting and no matter how hard you try to do everything right, you will screw up. Just recently, I was putting laundry away in Zach's room and I could hear him playing with Andrew in our bedroom, which is directly adjacent to his. Zach started playing with the heating vent in our room, which also happens to line up with the vent in his. "Stop playing with the vent, Zach," I heard Andrew say. Not even thinking, I leaned down and in a low but playful voice said, "Stop playing with the vent, Zach." My husband said Zach reacted as if a bolt of electricity had just shot through his tiny little body. He jumped in the air and started screaming, "It's a monster! It's a monster!" Andrew tried to calm him down and bring him into the room where I was, to show him that it was just Mommy, playing around and talking through the vent, but he refused. He's now convinced there is a monster living in his room.

"If you were trying to scare him," Andrew said later that night as we were getting ready for bed, "why didn't you do it from our room so he would think the monster lives in here? Maybe then we could reclaim our bed."

Without even trying, I somehow managed to help my son develop a fear of the dark, a belief in monsters and a phobia of heating vents. And he's only two. God only knows what other kinds of trauma I will unwittingly end up inflicting on him given some more time. Thankfully, babies don't remember the first few years of their life; it's nature's way of ensuring your children will talk to you in your retirement.

Anything muttered under your breath in the car will be repeated out loud somewhere else. My son must be the only two-year-old who announces his late arrival to Play School with the declaration, "No bloody parking!"

If Daddy enjoys having his dinner made for him every night by Mommy, he should never come home at the end of the day and comment, "I see the breakfast dishes are still on the table . . . what did you do all day?" And if Mommy would like to continue going out to her neighbourhood book club every Tuesday night, she should not hover over Daddy while he is feeding and changing the baby and announce, "You're doing it wrong!"

After the fifteenth consecutive repetition, neglecting to answer the questions: "What's that?" "Where's it going?" about the same object does not make you a bad mother.

What you may find endearing about your baby, others might consider simply annoying. Consider the teacher of my son's ballet class. After what I thought was a successful first session, I enrolled him in the class again. On the first day I did a quick survey of the room. "It looks like Zach is the only boy registered again," I com-mented. "Yes, well, I think your boy is all this class can handle, anyway," the teacher replied, adjusting a little girl's tutu. And here I thought the whole point of a ballet class for two-year-olds was to let them run around, jump and laugh, while music played in the background. I was too hurt to reply, but decided I wasn't going to spend a half hour of my time—time that I had paid for—trying to force my son to point his toes and bend his knees on command. Instead, right before the music started, I slipped Zach a couple of pieces of chocolate that I had stashed in my purse. Let's see if you can handle him now, I smirked to myself. Not everyone will appreciate a child's boundless energy and unique charms. But mommy will—sometimes.

Mothers, even when they are on their own, can easily be picked out of a lineup at the grocery store or the coffee shop. They are either looking frantically around, as if they've forgotten something (at least until they remember they left the baby with Grandma) or they are swaying slightly from side to side. It's like the phantom itch you experience if you lose a limb—you keep on rocking, even if you're not holding your baby.

It's perfectly acceptable to serve alcohol at a toddler's birthday party if parents are also attending. In fact, it's expected.

Mothers judge. You can instantly bond with another mother over the trials of child rearing, but silent appraisals happen all the time. I remember once being in the grocery store and arguing with Zach over a matchbox car. I had told him he could choose one car, since I had discovered the ninety-seven-cent investment would keep him quiet during my shopping trip. When he reached for a car that he happened to already have, I tried to get him to pick a different one. As he bellowed out his protest, a mother—accompanied by a very well-behaved little girl—pushed her cart past me, pursing her lips and shaking her head. "Fine," I said sternly. "If that is the way you are going to behave, you will not be getting a car." Given the other mother's reaction, I felt as if that was what was expected of me. But of course, I was the one who offered the car, and as I stood in the middle of the aisle, embarrassed and unable to quiet my son, it occurred to me that if he wanted to use his free car pass on one he already owned, who was I to argue? Either way, it was still going to cost me ninety-seven cents. So I waited until the lady turned the corner, then silently handed the car back to Zach, who immediately stopped screaming. On the other hand, I have also caught myself throwing disparaging glances at mothers who have neglected to properly address a playground infraction. Forget "all for one, and one for all," motherhood's motto should be, "judge not, lest you be judged."

If coffee changes colour when you put milk in it, it's not strong enough.

As soon as your baby is born, there is an intense pressure to document every moment of his life. This is impossible to maintain. Video recorders, digital cameras, baby albums, scrapbooks—I have one friend who started a baby blog before she even got pregnant. Meanwhile, I fight the guilt of the neglectful mother. I have at least five different baby albums and calendars that are largely empty after my son's first nine months. Once he started to crawl, if I put him down to file some new milestone or add a new picture, I couldn't find him again. It's much easier to record each significant moment with every new grey hair. That way, whenever you look in the mirror you will remember that, "this one is when he took his first step on his own, this one is when he choked on a piece of kiwi, this one is from the night I held him as he screamed in pain from his first ear infection...." And please, to all the scrap-booking fanatics, there are some things that do *not* need to be preserved for posterity—your baby's cord stump is one of them.

Society will never truly value the work of a stay-at-home mommy until society coughs up a paycheque. But we can ease the tension between mothers who stay at home and those who work outside the home by replacing the dreaded, "So, what do you do?" question, commonly heard at cocktail and dinner parties across the country, with the inquiry, "Where did you get those fabulous shoes?"

It's infinitely easier to discipline someone else's child in a calm and nurturing voice than it is to discipline your own.

If you want your baby to have a bowel movement, put him in a new diaper. Or his snowsuit.

Babies are not born cute. It takes at least three months before cute sets in. Some babies need even longer.

What doesn't kill you will make you stronger, but tripping over an errant pile of building blocks on your way down the stairs will leave you with a discernable limp for at least a week.

You will never be on time for anything, ever again. The effort and equipment required to travel with a baby means you need a day's advance notice just to leave the house for a quart of milk. Advice from well-meaning friends to prepare everything you need the night before (pack the diaper bag, put breakfast on the table, put the stroller in the car, put your baby to bed in the clothes he's going to wear the next day) is of little help. Having them come over to move the crib beside the front door—with your fully clothed baby inside and your espresso machine attached to the end—is infinitely more useful.

No, you can't use a CD player after a Fruit-to-Go snack has been shoved inside.

Motherhood is hazardous to your health. Babies can catch six to eight colds a year, and are ninety percent more likely to cough or sneeze just as you bend down to kiss them goodnight than they are lying in the crib on their own. A study in the *American Journal of Public Health* in 2003 found that mothers caring for their children more than twenty hours per week were one-and-a-half times more likely to have heart disease than women who don't provide care for children at all. Which makes sense since a mother's heart lurches and stops more often than that of a woman who doesn't spend her day yelling, "Oh my God! Get that out of your mouth!"

You will put something down, and then forget where it is. Luckily, a baby has strong lungs, so you can usually find him again.

You will feel like you're losing your mind, but if you hang out with other mothers, it's likely no one will notice. "I went to bed last night with my sunglasses on," said a friend of mine the other day. "Why?" I asked. "I don't know," she sighed. "It wasn't even sunny last night."

And the biggest truth about motherhood—the one we already know, but is so easy to forget—is that raising a child really will be the most important job you ever do.

(Oh, and one more: A bag of Oreo cookies is a completely acceptable way of dealing with the stress of the most important job you will ever do.)

Part IV
All in the Family

For Better or Worse

Mixing Marriage with Babies

Once upon a time there was a husband and wife who were deliriously in love. So delirious in fact that they said, "Let's start a family...."

"I'm sick of making dinner!" I said to my husband, throwing my *How to Be a Domestic Goddess* cookbook down on the table. "I may not be dressed in rags, but this Domestic Goddess is still a Cinderella. You're supposed to be my Prince Charming," I moaned. "So how come I'm still chained to the kitchen sink?"

"Because this isn't a fairy tale, darling," Andrew replied. "It's a marriage."

"I suppose you're right," I said, slumping over the kitchen table. "If marriage really were a fairy tale then you would have been the one who gave birth."

One of the reasons I married my husband was because he told me he used to be a chef. Well, he must have been the only chef who never used an oven, or a pot for that matter, or a pan. Maybe he was a virtual chef. Or maybe it was just a line he tossed out to lure me into bed. Come to think of it, I have also never seen the guitar he told me he used to play. Damn! I am such a sucker.

I'm not sure when the honeymoon stage ends, but I think it comes around the same time your baby hits the toddler years. Andrew and I never argued before we had a child. Now, sleep deprivation, a sporadic sex life, the pressure of responsibility and a baby who makes the Energizer Bunny look lazy have us snapping at each other like starved alligators at an all-you-can-eat buffet.

According to John Gottman—who studies the effect of parenthood on marriage, and is the director of the Relationship Research Institute in Washington—sixty-seven percent of couples experience "a significant drop in marital contentment after their first child is born," and new-parent couples apparently have eight times the number of arguments as non-parents. That's not very surprising, because really, what is there to argue about when you don't have children? Where should we go for dinner tonight? Do you think we have sex too often?

Like any baby, a marriage goes through its own kind of growing pains, but a dose of Infants' Tylenol is not going to stop you from waking up in the middle of the night screaming, "What is happening to us?"

When a couple gets married they make a decision to commit themselves to each other. When a couple has children they just go ahead and do it—and then ask to be committed later. Having a baby is a tremendous bonding experience, but there will still be times when you feel like you're starting to unhinge. Maybe couples wouldn't experience such a drop in marital contentment if wedding vows covered the stresses of parenthood. Maybe, before we chuck away the birth control, we should gaze deeply at each other and repeat the following vows:

Wife: I take you, my husband, to be my lawfully wedded partner in parenting. I promise to love you even when I hate you for leaving me alone all day with a toddler whose mood turns faster than the pages of a Harry Potter novel.

I will do my best not to resent the fact you are not physically tied to the baby, that your freedom has not been compromised, and that your body looks exactly the same as it did before we had a baby. I will try to remember that while you never prepare the meals for our baby, that you are quite aware he needs to eat and that the pressure of being the main breadwinner can be suffocating. I will try to refrain from snapping, "Did anyone rub snot on your shoulder today?" when you come home after a long day and complain of being tired.

I will let you develop your own parenting style; just because you don't do things my way doesn't mean you do things the wrong way. Okay, it does mean you do things the wrong way, but I will learn to hold my tongue.

Husband: I take you, my wife, to be my lawfully wedded partner in parenting. I will never forget the deep passion we first felt for each other, even when we're in a dry spell that lasts longer than a prairie winter. I promise to complement you, even when you're covered in baby sick and wearing the same track suit for the third straight day.

I will do my best to remember that you are dealing with a physical exhaustion I can't imagine, and that a tsunami of hormones floods you daily, creating a storm of emotions I often find perplexing. I will try to understand that while you agreed to stay at home to raise our baby, you will often experience moments of extreme self-doubt and frustration. And I will always be grateful that you gave me the best gift a man can ever have—a chance at a second childhood.

Together: We take each other—for better or worse—through sloppy kisses and first steps, sleep deprivation and dirty diapers, through the toddler years and, Lord help us, through adolescence.

Because love is what got us into this. And love is what will guide us through.

—26—

If It Takes a Village
The Importance of Grandparents

Some cultures believe it's strange if a child only has two parents. I'm beginning to discover what they mean. It's not until you have a child of your own that you realize the value of family and the importance of grandparents. Parenting books may offer advice, but a book won't move into the spare bedroom and take over the night shift so you can have eight hours uninterrupted sleep. A book won't play with your baby so you can have a shower. A book won't hold your hand and reassure you that everything is going to be okay when you confess you feel like you're falling apart. If it takes a village to raise a child, then it takes a village idiot to move thousands of miles away from the only people who will gladly offer free babysitting.

Luckily, even a cross-country commute won't keep grandparents away from the joy of reliving their own parenting experiences, free from the pressure of being responsible for the end product. My parents joke that if they knew how much fun grandchildren were going to be, they would have had them first. On a recent visit, as I watched them roll around on the floor with Zach, laughing and playing, pushing him on the park swing for hours and showering him with more toys than a Mattel warehouse could hold, a thought crossed my mind. If I knew how much fun grandparents were going to be, I would have had them first.

My parents, who have always advised me to spend money wisely, are now racking up outrageous long-distance phone bills while I try to coax a giggle or word out of their grandson. "Did you hear that, Grandpa?!" my mom will yell, even though he's sitting right beside her and the speaker phone. "He just said 'baaah'!"

My father, who has always been the stern disciplinarian, has suddenly turned into a six-foot teddy bear. My father—who required double bypass surgery after I pulled off the heads of his prized tulips when I was five because I was trying to "weed" the garden—is now telling me, "Honey, you've got to learn to relax. He's just a little boy. These things will pass."

My mother, who used to hover over me as a child, now admonishes me for being overprotective. When I tried to stop Zach from climbing over the vacuum cleaner at my parent's house last summer, she said, "Stop your fussing, he's having fun! Look at him, he's fascinated with it! He's obviously never seen one at your house before."

The birth of a grandchild seems to bring everything into focus, a perfect snapshot of lives lived and a life about to begin. And while a first-time parent is a new photo album, just waiting to be filled with memories and experiences, a grandparent is a library of memories and experiences that begs to be explored and shared. I'm sure it must be difficult for my parents to watch as my husband and I stumble along a path they have already walked— which must be why they toss out advice along the way, hoping to cushion a fall. I know they are just trying to help, so I've learned to stock their advice away like I would supplies of water and canned food in case of a natural disaster. I don't expect I will ever need it, but at least I know it's there in an emergency.

And while a baby may be the glue that bonds two parents together, a grandchild is the splint that repairs fractured relationships. When Andrew and I announced our engagement, my mother-in-law was not thrilled with the idea of a mixed marriage. Both our families are whiter than a loaf of Wonder Bread, but a Canadian daughter-in-law was twenty time zones away from the nice Kiwi girl-next-door they had envisioned for their first-born son. My husband and I were married four days after the ill-fated September 11, and my in-laws spent our wedding day at the Los Angeles airport. Having flown in from Auckland, they were unable to get a connecting flight to Toronto. They arrived the next day to see the caterers taking down the tent and cleaning up the last remains of an event celebrated without them; offering them further proof that nothing good can come from marrying a Canadian.

The distance between us finally began to thaw once our baby was born and it became clear that the only thing Zach had inherited from my side of the family was the sweater my grandmother knit for me when I was born. "I have produced a mini-version of you," I said to Andrew. "I really don't know what else I can do to make your mother like me." Apparently, that was all that was needed. We now have a much better relationship and talk regularly. I'm even lucky enough to get parenting advice from both sides of the globe.

I guess there's a price to pay for everything.

27

That's So SAHD
The Stay-at-Home Daddy

"If I could go through labour for you honey, I would. In an instant. Now don't forget to breathe."

If only science could make it so. As it stands, the most a woman in labour can hope for is that her husband will one day have to pass a seven-pound kidney stone. Nevertheless, a strange new phenomenon seems to be occurring in households across the country—daddies are offering to change positions with mommies, knowing that there is a damn good chance we may take them up on it.

According to Statistics Canada, the number of fathers taking parental leave increased from 3 percent in 2000 to 10 percent in 2001. Between 1991 and 2002, the number of stay-at-home dads increased from 88,000 to 110,000. The U.S. Census Bureau estimates that 98,000 fathers stay at home to look after their children full-time while their wives return to work. And the latest research out of the U.K. says that 155,000 men have assumed the role of full-time caregiver.

Fatherhood is hot—there's even a $1.6-million national study of male parenting happening at the University of Guelph in

Ontario. "Our goal is to bring fatherhood out of the shadows," says Kerry Daly, a professor at the university and co-chairman of the Father Involvement Research Alliance. According to Dr. Daly, societal expectations for fathers are so low that the news media often portrays involved fathers as heroes—suggesting that good fathers are the exception, not the norm.

The news media isn't alone in worshipping involved fathers. My husband worked from home for the first two years of our son's life before moving into an office. He wanted to fully experience those early days—when a baby's development happens faster than the time it takes to replace a roll of film. He is, in the eyes of my parents, a "Super Dad." I am just a mom. Or—as my dad introduced me on my wedding day—our son-in-law's wife.

"He's just so good with Zach," my mom said the last time my parents visited. "And so patient, don't you think, Grandpa?" she asked, watching from the kitchen window as Andrew played with Zach in the backyard.

"Especially with all he has to deal with," my dad replied, nodding in my direction.

"You do realize I'm still in the room, Dad?" I said from behind the newspaper I was reading.

While the number of men choosing parenthood over career is increasing, it is still considered an unconventional arrangement. Maybe that's because the acronym for stay-at-home dad is SAHD, and the male ego just can't handle that kind of job description. Or maybe it's because being a stay-at-home dad is dangerous work. Not only do you have to dodge temper-prone toddlers and the extra calories of half-eaten butter and jam sandwiches, but, according to the Framingham Heart Study, which is carried out in collaboration with Boston University in the United States, the risk of death is nearly twice that for stay-at-home dads as it is for dads who work out of home. Presumably, the realization of just how much laundry needs to be done in a week could cause a major heart attack.

And then, of course, there is the isolation. A friend of mine who is a stay-at-home dad complained that the mere presence of a SAHD is enough to launch a full-scale attack from SAHMS. "You become a walking therapy session for women at the community centre," he sighed when I asked him about his experiences. "You represent everything women love and hate about men. You become the target for all their resentments towards their husbands." Forget temper-prone toddlers, ducking female hostilities seems to be the biggest occupational hazard. "Men just aren't very social," my friend continued. "It isn't very manly to do more than grunt." And even when men do speak in multi-syllables, their attendance is merely tolerated at neighbourhood playgroups and Gymboree classes, or viewed as something of a novelty. "Being a new parent is difficult to begin with," he pointed out. "But if you mention how tough it is to a woman, you get a vindictive appreciation for your pain."

We women, it seems, can't make up our minds. We complain when fathers aren't involved with their children enough, or when they fail to help with the housework; but when we see a man attempting to break the status quo, we don't quite know what to do with him. It's like debating whether to wear thong underwear—will we love it, or will it just become a pain in the ass? And while mothers can expand their social network with outlets like postpartum classes and breast-feeding clinics, our biological differences make it impossible for men to create the type of quick bond that women can experience with each other. Things like cracked nipples and stretch marks unite mothers; it's just not natural for a man to understand, much less talk about, the mechanics of a breast pump.

Luckily, stay-at-home dads are proving resourceful, and a number of different organizations are sprouting up around the world where fathers can connect with each other over the joys of parenting. Manly or not, fathers are learning to support one another and even offer each other advice based on their collective experience. Like when one of my husband's friends—who had taken some personal leave when his son turned one so his wife could go back to work—commented to a group of other fathers that he didn't understand what his wife found so difficult, since his first week with the baby had gone smoothly. "Whatever you do, don't mention that to your wife!" was the quick and resounding response.

Hopefully, with more research projects like Dr. Daly's, the concept of fatherhood will continue to evolve. Perhaps stay-at-home moms will reach out to their fellow partners in parenting by bringing the sports section and stock market reports to drop-in playgroups, and perhaps more men will be encouraged to stay at home and raise their children.

After all, it really is in a mother's best interest to support full-time fatherhood. Men are, by nature, problem-solvers. And the more men we have at home all day, dealing with the domestic realities of raising a family, the greater the likelihood that somebody will finally invent a self-cleaning toilet and a ride-on vacuum cleaner.

28

You Turned Out Okay:
The Parenting Gap Between the Generations

"Here honey," my dad said, placing a steaming mug in front of me. "Have a cup of coffee." We were visiting my parents and I had just plunked myself down at the kitchen table with a yawn.

I sniffed the acrid, brownish brew suspiciously and asked, "Dad, when did you make this coffee?"

"It was fresh at six-thirty this morning," he replied.

"It's eleven-forty-five," I pointed out.

"Don't worry, I nuked it in the microwave for a minute before you came down."

I wonder how it is that my parents and I can share such similar experiences—like a passion for drinking coffee—yet never connect on what constitutes a proper cup. When I told my father I spent over $1,000 on an espresso machine he shook his head and told me I was being ridiculously extravagant. "What's wrong with Tim Horton's?" he asked, and I knew that even if I prepared him a lifetime of perfect cappuccinos I would never be able to bridge the gap between us. The way my parents and I view coffee is similar, I suppose, to how we view parenting. They can't understand why what has served them so well for so many years isn't good enough for me, and I can't convince them that my way may just be slightly more palatable.

I have always found it ironic that parents spend so much time and money on educating their children. At first, they brag to their friends about how smart you have become, but once you're old enough to offer opinions and suggestions on certain topics—like, for example, parenthood—suddenly you have no idea what you're talking about. If I try to talk to my parents about the differences in child rearing between our generations, they react as if I am accusing them of being negligent, which, in most cases, I am. Whenever I bring up any medical advances or thoughts on parenting that have occurred in the last thirty-four years, their answer is inevitably, "We never worried about that and you turned out okay." Which is interesting because I remember being asked repeatedly throughout my childhood, "What the hell is wrong with you?"

My friends and I commiserate about how hopelessly out of touch our parents are. One friend of mine recalled the time she phoned her mother in tears. She was having trouble nursing and wanted a sympathetic ear. Her mother, who lived across the country, jumped on the first plane out, armed with a breast-feeding manual.

"Mom," she complained when her mother handed it to her. "This book was published in 1971!"

"So?" she replied. "What do you think has changed?"

Meanwhile, our parents shake their heads and call us uptight—especially when it comes to things like food allergies. When Zach was ten months old we went to visit my parents for Christmas. I cleared out a shelf in their fridge, filled it with mommy-approved food, then posted a DO NOT FEED list on the door: "NO strawberries or honey; NO nuts; NO egg whites;

ABSOLUTELY NO salmon; NO tap water; ALL food to be cut up in small, non-chokeable pieces."

"Honestly," my father said after scanning the list—and the detailed CPR instructions and emergency numbers I had written beside it. "You kids are so paranoid. You had all that stuff, and you turned out okay. You don't have any allergies."

"You've got to be kidding me," my mother exclaimed when we went grocery shopping together. "Six dollars for a container of organic yogourt?! Are you insane? You never had any organic food when you were growing up, and you turned out okay."

I remember coming back after an afternoon of Christmas shopping during that visit to find my mother happily introducing Zach to his first taste of Cheerios. "Don't worry, there's a hole in the middle of them, so he won't choke," my mom assured me. I picked up the cereal box to do a quick inspection of the ingredients.

"HONEY NUT CHEERIOS?!?" I yelled out in horror, pointing frantically at the DO NOT FEED list on the fridge. "Are you trying to kill him?!"

Maybe it's the benefit of hindsight that allows grandparents to relax; knowing that even though they drove us around without car seats, put us to sleep in cribs painted with lead, fed us non-organic food and neglected to spend every minute of the day supervising our play and stimulating our minds, we survived. On a recent family vacation my husband, Zach and I were holed up with my parents in a hotel room waiting for an early morning flight from Toronto to Barbados where we were going to celebrate my father's sixty-fifth birthday. Andrew was taking the luggage to the lobby and I had just come out of the bathroom to find my parents sitting on the couch watching cartoons. Zach was nowhere in sight. Following the muffled giggles of "Help!" I found him stuck under the bed playing with an empty Bic lighter that must have been left behind by a previous guest.

"Mom! Dad!" I screamed. "Weren't you watching him?! He's playing with a lighter for Christ's sake!"

"What are you so upset about?" my dad said. "He didn't start a fire did he?"

"Really, Dorianne," my mom added. "You need to learn to relax."

Rescuing Zach from under the bed—and a possible future as a pyromaniac—it occurred to me that I have a much different perspective on the benefits of my parent's hindsight. I obviously only survived my childhood out of sheer luck.

I wonder what the real issue is. Is parenting really so much harder now, or do we just have too much information at our disposal? My father, who always directed me to "look it up," if I had a question about something, now claims I read way too much about parenting. "Why don't you just trust your instinct with Zach?" he asked me once. "Or is there not a book that tells you how to do that?"

No doubt there have been great advances in what we know about things like SIDS and how to prevent it, but as a result, we now spend the first six months of our babies' lives in perpetual panic. When Zach was eleven days old, we took him on his first outing to the local coffee shop. I was sitting inside with my husband, my mother and a friend, trying to enjoy a celebratory triple-shot cappuccino, when I noticed a man smoking. All my parenting books had warned that exposure to second-hand smoke was the leading cause of SIDS. I instantly panicked and tried to shield Zach from the smoke. "Oh my God!" I whispered to my mother, "Do you think Zach will be okay? Do you think the smoke is going to affect him?"

"You can't be serious," she replied. "The guy is fifteen feet away—and he's outside."

"It's dangerous for a baby to be around smoke!" I snapped as I grabbed a receiving blanket and draped it over Zach's car seat, forcing him to spend his world debut staring at a boring piece of fabric, and most likely wondering why he had even bothered to make the trip down the birth canal into the real world if this was going to be all he got to see.

The very next day my mother and I had a terrible fight over a pacifier. I was adamant that no child of mine would *ever* use a pacifier—my library of experts had advised against it. My mother was adamant a pacifier would end my son's three-hour crying jag.

"The child needs a soother," my mother told me.

"I'm not giving him a soother!" I said firmly, a note of disdain in my voice. "All the books say don't give him a soother! My son will never have a soother!"

"I don't care what the books say," my mother replied dismissively. "He's not hungry; he just needs something to suck on to calm him down. You had a soother until you were three, and you turned out okay." We argued back and forth until, out of desperation, I grabbed a pacifier—which had magically appeared out of my mother's purse, sterilized and ready to use—and popped it into Zach's mouth. And then I started to cry. I felt like I had broken some cardinal parenting rule by giving in; that, after only two weeks, I was already a terrible mother. And then my mother started to cry. She had never wanted to impose her parenting beliefs on me, she had only wanted to help. And there we sat in the nursery, the two of us sobbing and apologizing to each other, while Zach, quiet at last, happily sucked away on his soother.

"Oh, Mom!" I cried. "How am I going to do this? I don't know how to be a mother."

"Don't worry," she said, patting my hand and wiping a tear away with her sleeve. "I had no idea what I was doing in the beginning either. And you turned out okay."

It's true that we now read and know more about parenting than our parents ever did; these days, cigarettes even come with a government health warning about the dangers of smoking around newborns. But even with all our newfound knowledge, what we really need is a government warning about parenthood:

"Caution: Too much information about parenting may cause unnecessary levels of fear and anxiety. Stop reading stuff on the Internet. You turned out okay."

29

The Grocery Store and Other Nervous Breakdowns

Is Daddy a Better Mommy than Me?

I have come to the conclusion that my husband and I are not raising the same son. Or else he's taking someone else's son to the grocery store.

"That's it!" I said to Andrew the other day, dumping the grocery bags on the kitchen table. "I am never taking Zach grocery shopping again! We can live on takeout."

"What happened this time?" my husband sighed as he started unpacking the food.

The same thing that happens every time I take him out, I fumed to myself. If he's not on the floor whirling around in some sort of toddler breakdance fever, he's either poking his fingers into vegetables, screeching, "I want a cookie!" or racing through the aisles like Hurricane Kellogg, leaving a trail of fallen cereal boxes behind him.

"Look!" I said, waving a home delivery service flyer in Andrew's face. "The cashier handed me this on the way out!"

"Dealing with these kinds of things is what being a mother is all about," my husband laughed, coming towards me to give me a hug.

"And just what is being a father all about?" I asked, pushing him away.

"Well, the same thing," he replied.

"Oh, really? Because I didn't see you in aisle seven!"

Ever since Zach hit the "terrible twos"—which started at about fourteen months—I feel like I have been running on a treadmill to the madhouse: I never seem to get there, but I know it's in front of me, just waiting. My husband doesn't understand because Zach figured out months ago whose buttons were more fun to push. Unlike me, Andrew has never experienced the public humiliation of trying to negotiate with a two-year-old who is holding his sanity hostage.

"Maybe it's something you're doing," my husband suggested. "Zach always knows if he acts up with me, we'll come straight home. Do you do that?"

"No," I shot back. "If I came straight home as soon as he acted up we would never make it out the front door."

"Well, maybe he picks up on the fact you're more anxious. Maybe you should . . . umm, you know . . . relax a little."

"*Relax*?" I asked incredulously. "I AM RELAXED!"

I know, who am I kidding? I can't relax; I'm a mother. I don't have the energy to relax. But what I can't understand is how, after seeing my transformation into a mother, my husband has been able to remain so laid back. He doesn't worry about his skills as a father. He doesn't hover over our son. When he came home one day after a trip to the park, boasting about how Zach had gone down the spiral slide on his own for the very first time, I freaked. "You let him go down the spiral slide on his own? Are you crazy?"

"No," he shrugged, unsure what all the fuss was about. "But my wife is."

He doesn't start his sentences with, "I feel like I'm a terrible mother. . . ." He doesn't berate himself for yelling too loudly at

Zach; he apologizes and moves on. He doesn't feel guilty for working or taking time for himself; he knows he spends quality time with his family whenever he can.

He never imagines worst-case scenarios. When I asked him to fix the railings on our back deck because I was certain they were too far apart and posed a definite baby hazard, he said, "It's fine, I measured the railings the other day. Zach's head might squeeze through but his shoulders are too wide to let him fall." But I'm a mother. I know that the head is the biggest part of the body—once that makes it through, everything else slips out pretty easily.

He doesn't lie awake at night thinking of the time when I lost sight of our son at the gym—a sickening, split-second moment that, even though months have passed since it happened, is still as intensely frightening as it was that day.

After almost two-and-a-half years he still has no idea how to pack the diaper bag properly, and the only time he remembers to take it with him is if he trips over it on his way out the door. And he still thinks that, when it comes to clothing, red and purple go together and a checkered T-shirt complements striped pants.

I don't understand why he can't parent more like me; and in the same instant, I find myself wishing I could parent more like him.

I think we must be suffering from a lack of communication. I make a point of telling my husband how to do everything. But whenever he offers an opinion, it's like pissing on a live wire. I feel myself begin to twitch and then sparks start shooting from my mouth. I expect him to be a full partner in parenting, but when he does manage to develop his own style and—despite my constant presence and influence—foster a unique relationship with our son, I find myself surprised.

A few weeks ago, he asked me if I could go to the bank for him. It's a job he normally reserves for Saturday mornings so he and Zach can go together. It was a beautiful day so I walked down to our local branch with Zach in tow. I wanted to save myself some time so I avoided the tellers my husband usually goes to and headed straight for the automatic banking machines near the entrance.

"Toys!" Zach cried out in delight, struggling to climb out of his stroller.

Thinking he was referring to the toy store, conveniently located next to the bank, I said gently, "No honey, we're not buying any toys today. Mommy just has to make a quick deposit and transfer and then we'll go home."

"TOYS!!" he said with increasing urgency.

"Zach! Please sit down," I pleaded. "I'll just be a minute. Here's one of your trucks to play with."

"NO!" he yelled, and shot it across the floor. "TOYS!!"

I hoisted him out of the stroller with one arm, while trying to collect my card, wallet and deposit slip with the other. I grabbed his hand to lead him out of the bank but he collapsed on the floor in an angry blur of flailing arms and legs, screaming out his plea for "TOYS!" Pushing the stroller ahead of me and dragging my son behind me I left the bank, embarrassed and angry that I had no control over my son's behaviour and acutely aware that my slack parenting skills were now being captured on a security camera— most likely to end up as a clip on a *Dr. Phil* parenting special: "What Are Parents Doing Wrong These Days? Are You Raising a Serial Killer?"

When I told my husband what happened, he said, "That's odd. He never has a tantrum when I take him. Did you let him play with the toys around the corner, the ones by the teller's desk?"

A week later I was forced to call Andrew from my cell phone while stuck in a traffic jam. Shouting to be heard over the wails of, "I want Daddy's helicopter song! SING THE HELICOPTER SONG!!" coming from the backseat, I found myself begging for the lyrics to some imaginary song he had invented. I ended up just handing the phone back to Zach who immediately calmed down once he heard daddy sing, "Helicopter, helicopter, please come down, we're two rhinoceroses stuck on the ground . . ."

It was then that I finally realized we were, in fact, raising the same son; we just weren't doing it together. We were both searching for ways to be the best mommy and daddy we could be, but we had neglected to share what we had discovered. My husband and I will never parent the same way, and why should we expect to? Combined, we can make the perfect parent—the yin to the other's yang—with all our flaws and strengths.

And the best part is, I'm starting to learn from my husband. For example, I have finally managed to unravel the mystery of why it takes a million sperm to reach one egg! All I had to do was observe him staring straight into the fridge, declaring that he can't find the milk, even if it happens to be the only thing in there.

And, I have noticed that on the rare occasions when my husband does lose his cool, I instantly relax. See, I can do it.

Part V

Everything I Know I Learned
from Baby Einstein

30

My Son and the TV

Only One Turns Off

"This chapter was made possible with the kind assistance of the Treehouse Network and the Baby Einstein Company."

I was at a playgroup recently when the conversation turned to babies and television. "I never let my baby watch TV," said one mother.

"We don't even own a television!" piped in another.

Suddenly I found myself feeling isolated and inadequate, surrounded by mothers who had obviously never caught themselves humming the theme song from *Bear in the Big Blue House*.

But then I realized something: almost every mother in that room was planning on going back to work once her maternity leave was up, which would eliminate the need to let your baby watch a half hour of TV. At work, co-workers don't tug on your pant leg, pleading, "Up Mommy!" while you try to sip your coffee. Co-workers don't toss Bob the Builder figurines into your mug. Co-workers don't chuck your sugar cubes in the toilet.

My mother's generation never felt guilty about parking their babies in front of *Sesame Street*. Maybe it was because there weren't any experts to tell them they shouldn't. They welcomed Big Bird and Cookie Monster into their homes and celebrated children's television for what it was intended to be—a chance to go to the bathroom unaccompanied.

Not that I would ever advocate using television as a babysitter. I would hope a babysitter would stop my son from climbing on top of the coffee table to get a better view. I would hope that a babysitter would be able to grab the remote control before he buried it in my potted plant. No, I use TV more as a life preserver, to keep me afloat when I feel like I'm drowning under the pressure of keeping a baby entertained for the majority of the day.

I have to admit, there is a part of me that feels like I'm shirking my responsibilities as a mother when I let Zach watch television. But that part of me usually isn't awake at five a.m. when he cries out from the nursery, refreshed and ready to tackle a new day. I stumble downstairs, pop in a *Baby Einstein* video, collapse on the couch and tune out any guilt I might be feeling over slack parenting skills. I know he is enjoying much more stimulating company than I could ever provide at that hour.

But really, why should I feel so bad? The Baby Einstein Company sells an estimated $17 million of products a year, and that's not all to me. I do believe—in moderation and in the right context—children's videos and TV can promote early learning. I see it in Zach when he laughs out loud at the sounds, colours and movements he sees on the screen, points out objects like a cow or truck, and hums to the music.

Of course, TV does have its downsides. My sister's first complete sentence was, "Come on down, you're the next contestant on the *Price is Right!*" And my cousin's six-year-old daughter recently told her, "Mommy, if you were murdered, I would find out who did it," after her grandmother let her watch an episode of *Cold Case*.

But I monitor what Zach watches. I don't turn on *Days of Our Lives*, or the *Teletubbies* when he's around. One is inappropriate, and the other is ... well, it's just plain disturbing.

The American Academy of Pediatrics recommends no television whatsoever for children under age two. "In contrast to the way real life unfolds and is experienced by young children, the pace of TV is greatly sped up," says Dr. Dimitri Christakis, whose study for the Academy claims that watching videos as a toddler may lead to attention deficit disorder.

Well, Dr. Christakis obviously never spent an afternoon chasing after my toddler, because real life unfolds pretty damn fast when you're trying to keep up with a two-year-old. Besides, I've come to terms with the fact that a baby who only sleeps around four hours every night most likely already has a short attention span.

Some scientists suggest that TV viewing hinders a baby's development and causes obesity and lethargy later in life. But to tell you the truth, I'm not really worried that Zach will turn into a couch potato—he doesn't sit still long enough to sprout roots. What I'm more worried about is the effect children's television is having on me. It's like a drug that takes the edge off adult life: I would rather watch a cartoon turtle and bear argue over who gets to play with the soccer ball than the depressing reality of the evening news.

I suppose admitting to the problem is the first step towards recovery. When Zach's napping I'll close the blinds and quickly turn on the Treehouse Network to get my daily fix. I need to find out if Sister Bear is going to stand up to the peer pressure from the other girl bears; how the new racoon will make friends at Timothy's school; whether Bob will finish the job. Will Ruby lay off Max and just let him keep the damn frog in his pocket? Do the Mole Sisters come to terms with the fact that they are just moles? Will Big Bear get any mail today? Does Dora find her backpack?

What are the Rubberdubbers up to, and just what kind of medication are those two crazy women who host Treehouse on anyway?

No, I'm not worried about the amount of television Zach watches, but I definitely need to pull the plug.

31

Jingle Bells

Reliving the Joy of Christmas Through a Child's Eyes

Only twenty-six more sleeps until Christmas!

I don't understand why some people find Christmas so stressful. Stressful is running through the reception area of your local gym after a Baby Bubbles swim class—in your underwear—hysterically yelling out your son's name, because in the two seconds it took to grab your pants from the locker he managed to dart out of the change room and make a beeline for the front door. But being forced to eat too much and to shop for the entire month of December? Throw in one too many rum and eggnogs and that's my idea of heaven.

Christmas has always been my favourite time of year. I start humming "Jingle Bells" in September and stringing Christmas lights the day after Halloween. I have memorized all the lines from *It's a Wonderful Life*. I get teary when I see a nativity scene or hear "I'll Be Home for Christmas." I order a gingerbread latte from Starbucks just so I can get a red holiday cup. My husband is afraid if I catch him sitting still long enough I'll sprinkle him with tinsel and tape a gift tag to his head. Last week, after I strapped an electric

Rudolph nose and a pair of antlers on Zach, Andrew threatened to find a twelve-step program for Christmas junkies. He shouldn't bother: there's no shaking this elf off my back.

This Christmas, my jingle fever is worse than usual because this is the first year Zach will be old enough to participate in the festivities. This is the first year I can dope him up on sugar before I unleash him on a room full of relatives—which should, at the very least, get them to stop asking when number two is coming along. And this is the first year he will be able to squeal with delight as he rips into a present (by the way Santa, it had better be a wooden train set).

Every family has their holiday traditions—like the annual Sager budget meeting. The first weekend after Thanksgiving, my father pulls out graphs and spreadsheets charting the steady stream of money out of his retirement fund, and religiously repeats to deaf ears, "We're not going overboard on Christmas this year." And every year we go overboard—it's tradition. But this year is the first time that my husband and I, as parents, can start creating our own holiday traditions—the ones that will define our family and how we rejoice in the season. This will also be the year that my mother and father, as grandparents, redefine overboard.

One of my most vivid memories of Christmas was the year I was five. I had worked myself into a state because our house didn't have a chimney and I was sure Santa wouldn't be able to deliver all those presents I had earned with months of good behaviour. I went to bed on Christmas Eve like a sad little puppy dog, my tail between my legs and my chin dragging on the ground. When Christmas morning arrived, I jumped out of bed as my mom called for me from downstairs. She was standing by the front door, shivering in her nightgown, as snow billowed into the hallway. "Look!" she yelled out. "The front door was left open last night! This must be how Santa got into the house!"

The tree was bulging with a pile of brightly wrapped treasures, and while I can't remember a single present I opened that day, I will never forget the magic I felt—that giddy, breathless excitement that is as fleeting as childhood. Santa was real and presents did just appear. Life was good. As the years passed I held onto that memory, as if it were a precious ornament wrapped in tissue paper and carefully protected from the grumbles of people who said the true meaning of Christmas had been bought out by greed and consumerism.

They're missing the point, I would think to myself. You don't need Christmas to practise peace on earth and goodwill towards men; life presents us with thousands of opportunities throughout the year to do that. What Christmas gives us is one day to remember what it was like to be a child; to have your sense of wonder indulged. It's one day when you can forget the fragile nature of life and believe in magic again. And that is the gift I am looking forward to unwrapping this year—that and a full night's sleep. Or a new espresso machine—whatever's easiest, Santa.

32

Climbing the Ladder
Competitive Parenthood

Parenthood is an equal-opportunity employer. It allows the incompetent to mingle with the overachievers, and the smug the chance to socialize with the humble. You can't get promoted or fired, and retirement isn't an option, so competency is not really a required job skill. Nonetheless, staying ahead of the pack is a vicious rat race.

I'm only a little more than two years into this job and the overtime is already killing me. There are schedules to keep and milestones to reach. Activities must be planned and stimulation encouraged because, according to scientists, 75 percent of a person's brain development occurs between birth and the age of three. That's a lot of pressure for parents, especially considering that, for the first year, you are so exhausted the most stimulation you can offer is asking the baby if he remembers where you put your car keys. And for the second and third years, you're too busy running after him to worry about whether he's being stimulated properly. You do, however, spend a great deal of time during these years developing your baby's imagination by threatening some sort of dire punishment as you constantly repeat, "I will count to three, mister, but trust me, you do not want me to get to three!" You have no idea what you would do if you ever reached three, but you hope your baby's ability to figure that one out lies somewhere in the remaining 25 percent of his undeveloped brain.

When I left the career track for the mommy track I was looking forward to a more relaxing vocation. That was before I spent entire days trying to come up with different ways to nurture my baby's intelligence. And apparently, I have some major catching up to do. During my pregnancy, my sole preparation for parenthood was to increase my calorie intake. I treated that time of pre-parenthood much like I did my school exams: I did minimal preparation beforehand, preferring to cram in everything I felt I would need to know the night before the big test. If all else failed, I figured I could always bluff my way through. Meanwhile, all the other mothers I have met spent their nine months of pregnancy reading to their womb and piping in Mozart, which means my baby is already woefully behind—although he was born with the exceptional ability to call my bluff.

Parenthood these days has become an intensive occupation focused on developing the über-baby. Companies like Smart Start Baby, Brighter Child, Baby Einstein, Brainy Baby and Creative Wonder offer a range of infant and toddler developmental and educational toys that fill up any potential downtime. These manufacturer's have somehow convinced parents that a "smart" toy like a multi-sensory rattle in primary colours is much better for a baby's emerging brain potential than a "dumb" toy like, say, an empty carton of pizza, when really, the only difference between the two is about forty dollars and a good marketing plan. Imagine if a pizza carton came with a gold seal stating, "Baby tested, mother approved—especially when delivered with extra pepperoni!" It could also include testimonials: "Four corners introduce baby to geometric shapes!" "Grease spots arranged in visually stimulating patterns!" "Lingering anchovy aroma encourages sensory stimulation!" "Guaranteed to provide as much—even more—stimulating play than any other baby toy on the market!" "Purchase price includes the cost of dinner!" With the right kind of promotion, parents wouldn't worry so much that, inevitably, a baby will find a pizza carton far more interesting than a pile of expensive toys designed to enhance his intelligence.

Luckily, if the toys fail to make a dent in our children's brain development, there are a number of stimulating activities on offer that, if nothing else, will ensure parents never have any free time again. Baby Sign Language, Kinder Music, Mother Goose, Baby Bubbles, Toddler Ballet, Tumble Class, Gymboree . . . at two-and-a-half, my son has a more active social life than any adult I know.

But, according to John Bruer, author of *The Myth of the First Three Years: A New Understanding of Early Brain Development and Lifelong Learning*, parents should relax. Apparently, there is no good neuroscientific evidence to support the theory that the experiences of a child's first three years will profoundly affect or determine brain development. Which is good to hear, because my son and I desperately need a break. Near the end of one of Zach's ballet classes, he collapsed on the floor in an exhausted little heap, looked up at me and sighed, "Wanna watch some TV?"

But what if John Bruer is wrong? As it stands, parents don't want to risk wasting those three precious years of brain development on free time, or an empty pizza carton—unless you want your poor baby to grow up delivering them for a living. So we continue to whip out flash cards, sign our babies up for art classes and discuss the benefits of toys that focus on the right side of the brain versus the left side without asking ourselves one very important question: Do we really want a super-intelligent child? One who doesn't just suspect that mommy and daddy have no idea what they're doing, but who knows *for certain*?

Of course, raising a prodigy is not the only occupational hazard this job presents; first you need to survive the aggressive one-upmanship of early parenthood. If you think fighting a rival colleague for a promotion is a cut-throat business, then you have never sat in a Gymboree class with a group of other mothers, competing over how many bowel movements your baby has in a day.

I remember how, during my son's first year, I would worry if he seemed to be lagging behind other babies, and how I would secretly crow when he appeared to be surpassing his peers. When Zach scored in the ninetieth percentile on the growth chart at twelve weeks, it was like he aced the entrance exam to law school. "Every baby develops differently," I would reassure the other mothers at playgroup as they anxiously compared their baby's growth to mine, all the while enjoying the silent triumph of knowing that Zach had obviously left the others crawling in his dust.

"The ninetieth percentile, eh?" said a friend. "That's great. Sam scored in the ninety-eighth last week.... But don't worry," she added hastily, after scaling my victory to plant her own flag—eight percentage points ahead of mine. "Every baby develops differently."

I've seen mothers act like drill sergeants, shooting out questions about the number of hours your baby sleeps, the food he eats, the words he has spoken, when he crawled, when he walked, how many teeth he has. It's like mothers keep mental graphs where they can jot down all this information next to their own baby's achievements. We may not be able to remember to buy milk for three days in a row, but we can certainly keep track of the exact day the baby next door hit a milestone before our own.

And then there are the mothers who are slightly more subtle; who are no less competitive, but whose successes are scored in other parent's failures. When I confessed to a friend—whose daughter is a few months younger than Zach—that I felt like I was headed towards a nervous breakdown after two years of sleep deprivation, she replied, "I'm sorry, but I just can't relate. Our daughter is such a good little sleeper. I just adore being a mother; I guess I don't find motherhood to be as difficult as you do."

"Maybe you should try letting him cry it out," she suggested. "I hear that works."

I would have invited her over at three in the morning to demonstrate how well letting a toddler cry it out at night actually works—especially once he's old enough to yell out, "I want my mommy!" for forty-five minutes straight—but my head had already fallen into my coffee cup.

Perhaps the competitive nature of parenting, and the desire to create an exceptional child, comes from the pressure mothers put on themselves to excel at this job we have undertaken. It makes raising a child seem more like detonating a bomb: one wrong move and it could all blow up in your face.

Mothers may be busy creating baby geniuses, but what we don't seem to understand is that the more competitive motherhood gets, the harder it becomes to talk about how difficult motherhood can be. Parenthood can be a minefield of potential hazards and missteps and often, it seems, the only way parents can judge their own performance is to compare and criticize that of others. But if we become too concerned with surpassing each other, there is no one left to lean on.

There's no "I" in teamwork—or parenthood for that matter. We need to stick together! After all, if these activities and educational toys really do make our babies smarter, then our little Einsteins are soon going to realize they are the ones teaching us. And when that happens, parenthood really will be an equal-opportunity employer—we'll all be screwed.

33

My Essentials:

Buying for Baby

A month before our baby was due Andrew was working on the family budget, trying to determine just how expensive this little adventure into parenthood was going to be. "That's not so bad," he smiled, shutting down his Excel spreadsheet. "We'll need a crib, a stroller, a car seat, of course, and some diapers."

And then I handed him my list of baby essentials—all three pages of it. His face went pale as he scanned the list and foresaw the money draining from his wallet. "You realize you're only giving birth to one baby," he said, "not the entire maternity ward."

I suppose he had a point. But while the thought of impending parenthood can cause some panicked purchases, I'm certainly not the only one shopping. According to a survey by Prudential in the U.K., British parents spend an estimated £446 million on baby clothes and accessories for children in the first year of life. That's approximately $998 million. I haven't racked up nearly that amount of damage, I pointed out to Andrew. "It's only a matter of time," I heard him mutter under his breath.

Mothers aren't completely impractical, however. While I have one friend who will gladly blow seventy dollars on a new pair of shoes for her toddler, she won't spend more than twenty on a pair for herself. And another mother I know stopped purchasing any children's clothes that cost more than fifteen dollars once she realized how ridiculous it was to buy a designer baby outfit that you end up covering with a five dollar bib from Wal-Mart.

No matter how much you exhaust your credit card in preparation for life with a baby, every parent will inevitably compile a list of baby essentials that prove to be as much use as Britney Spears at a neuro-physicist conference. Like the expensive pack of Pee-pee Teepees I bought to prevent unexpected showers during a diaper change. I quickly learned that it was just easier to keep my mouth closed until the new diaper was securely on. And that odd-looking nasal aspirator: are we really supposed to use it to suck mucus out of our poor baby's nose? I thought it was a baster for a tiny turkey. Come to think of it, I should add Zach's crib to our list. If we'd known how little time he was actually going to spend sleeping in it, we could have saved our money and splurged on a king-size bed for the whole family instead.

Of course, every parent has a few favourite essentials that they truly would not have been able to survive without, like my two choices below.

Baby Transport

There are a number of different modes of transport for a baby: the baby car seat, the baby backpack, the Baby Björn and the baby sling. All of which are designed to get mommy and baby to the same destination—the coffee shop.

But probably the most expensive purchase a new parent will make is the stroller—the one piece of equipment that will reveal your yearly take-home pay faster than the car you drive. I remember rationalizing with my husband over this purchase. I reasoned that spending a small fortune on a stroller would be worth it since we would be sure to use it for the next baby, making what might seem like a rather large expense appear more like a sound financial decision. Three strollers, and still only the same baby later, I discovered that strollers are like computers—as soon as you buy one it's obsolete. The next model up is already in the works, with a whole bunch of upgrades that weren't available with yours. And of course, things like extra large shopping baskets or detachable toddler trays won't work properly with your particular operating system. Besides, very few strollers can be used for all situations. I realized this after I took my newborn shopping in my brand new three-wheeler, all-terrain vehicle. I had just made my way to the escalator that led up to the shopping mall and briefly considered taking the stairs, which seemed to be the fastest route. Once I came to my senses, I tried to back up and manoeuvre the whole production towards the elevator. In the process, I accidentally pressed the emergency stop button with the stroller's large, protruding front wheel and the escalator was brought to a grinding halt.

Surviving the grunts and accusing glances of shoppers who were forced to hike two flights up to the mall was only half as embarrassing as trying to corner the aisles in all the stores. It was like driving a Zamboni in an icebox. I decided I could either avoid shopping until my son learned to walk, or I could shell out the money for a sleek and compact umbrella stroller—the sports car to my SUV.

Of course, the most important thing to remember when buying a stroller is that a baby will eventually be using it—smearing food over it, spilling juice on it and spitting up all over the upholstery. And no matter how much money you spend on a stroller, nothing will prevent mildew from growing on it if you fold it up when it's damp, which, if you live in Vancouver, is just about every time you go out.

Baby Monitor

The baby monitor (or, electronic umbilical cord) is a valuable life-line for new mommies—even better than satellite television at three in the morning. It was the only way I could manage to use the bathroom on my own or grab a nap without panicking that the baby had suddenly stopped breathing.

Almost two and a half years have passed and I still sleep with the monitor beside my pillow, which of course is completely unnecessary since even our neighbours can hear Zach when he wakes up at night. But on those occasions when he is sleeping soundly—and I remember both of them—I cling to the monitor, terrified that he has stopped breathing, but even more terrified that if I go in to check on him, he'll wake up.

Not long ago, I discovered that our monitor was picking up reception from the rest of the neighbourhood when, after Zach had happily crawled into our bed one morning, I could still hear a baby crying. At first I thought it was a definite sign that two years of broken sleep had finally caused me to lose my mind. But then I heard a voice: "Good morning my little darling, did you have a nice sleep?" and I knew for certain that the voice was not coming from inside my head, or from anywhere inside my house. For one, my husband and I never sound that chirpy in the morning unless we're on our third espresso. And two, we have never had to ask our son if he had a good sleep, because the answer is always no.

Besides, any question regarding the quality of my son's sleep would be muttered from underneath him, since most mornings I wake up to find myself with half his body flung over the top of my head.

Even in the two years since our son was born, baby monitors have become increasingly high-tech. Take, for example, the Fisher-Price Calming Vibrations Monitor. It offers a remote control so you can listen and respond to your baby with calming vibrations and soothing sounds through a crib attachment. This is presumably easier than shaking your husband awake and convincing him it's his turn to go rock the baby back to sleep.

Or, the Anglecare Movement Sensor Monitor, which monitors your baby's breathing and movements through a sensor pad you place under his body. If the sensor doesn't detect any movement, an alarm goes off to let parents know that the baby may have stopped breathing. According to a friend (who eventually returned hers after her stress levels reached a dangerously high level) the more likely explanation is that the baby simply rolled off the sensor pad. Apparently, the Anglecare monitor has allowed parents the freedom to stop creeping into the baby's room every five minutes to hover over the crib, staring anxiously at the baby to make sure he's still breathing. Now, parents can remain in the living room, where they can stare anxiously at the monitor. It is estimated that these new monitors have cut clandestine trips to the nursery by at least 5 per cent.

The monitor I wish we had known about when we went shopping for baby supplies is the Graco Family Listen 'n' Talk Monitor. It has a walkie-talkie feature that allows parents to listen and talk to each other from across the house. So if you're downstairs taking a much needed rest and your husband goes upstairs to change the baby, instead of just sitting there wondering if he's doing it right, you can radio up instructions like, "Remember, if the baby has soaked through his diaper, you need to change the sheet in the crib. You can't just move him to a dry patch!"

I know that I will eventually have to cut the cord; the range on these things will never be strong enough to cover the distance between my bedroom and Zach's dorm room at university. And, much to my disappointment, even after leaving the monitor on all day long to pick up different dispatches, it is clear that the only day-time soap operas being played out in my neighbourhood are on *Days of Our Lives.*

Although I did catch a snippet of conversation the other day when I heard someone complain, "Are they ever going to get that boy to sleep through the night?"

Not likely. But stay tuned.

−34−

Potty Training
A Work in Progress

Dr. Phil claims he can potty train a child in one day. It's a boast that sounds a lot like the claim a woman can have multiple orgasms; I'm sure it's true, but I have yet to meet a woman who has experienced it.

I have bought a potty for Zach, but that's as far as I have gotten—so this chapter is a work in progress. There are an amazing variety of potties on the market, all very cute and colourful. It almost makes you forget that you are shopping for a receptacle for your baby's waste products that will undoubtedly end up sitting in your kitchen or living room. I opted for just a plain potty instead of one of the fancier versions that sing when you do your business. The poor kid already thinks voices come out of the heating vents, I don't want to develop another phobia. So far, Zach really hasn't shown much interest in the potty, other than to take the splash-guard out and use it as a ramp for his matchbox cars. But I've been getting a kick out of it. I put the training seat on our toilet when my girlfriends who don't have kids come to visit. "Oh my God!"

one cried out when she came into the kitchen after using the bathroom, "When did my ass get so big?!"

Maybe I'm reluctant to start potty training because I can't bear the thought of my little baby being so independent—so grown up. Or, maybe it's because one of my parenting books says that, when you train boys, they often like to play with their feces, and will sometimes even smear it over the walls. I really don't think I'm ready to redecorate.

But there's still plenty of time. Boys take longer I've been told, and Zach doesn't start preschool for another six to eight months. The real potty panic won't start until about two weeks before he's due to enrol. I do know a mother whose son is the same age as Zach, and she claims he just woke up one day and potty trained himself. He even wakes up in the middle of the night to use the potty, cleans his hands and then tucks himself back into bed. Amazing. Did I mention this same boy has slept soundly for twelve hours every night from the day he was born? Naturally.

Apparently I wasn't trained until I was almost three. My grandmother was visiting and I came down the stairs with a diaper in my hand and lay down beside my mother. "That child needs to be trained," my grandmother declared. My parents left me with her for the weekend; when they came back, I was trained.

It sounds like a pretty foolproof method to me. The next time we visit my parents, maybe Andrew and I will take off for a few nights and let Grandma and Zach spend some quality time over the potty.

She mentioned recently it was about time for new wallpaper.

35

It Can Always Get Worse

The Effects of Sleep Deprivation, Part II

I cut myself the other day while I was slicing a bagel. I bled espresso.

When my son was fifteen months old and my husband and I were struggling with sleep deprivation, the one thing that kept me going—my small ray of hope—was that Zach would eventually fall into a pattern that mimicked the rest of normal society. He is now two-and-a-half, and I can no longer remember how normal society functions.

"We have to remain positive!" Andrew told me, grabbing on to my shoulders and shaking me into survival mode, like we were two starving, dehydrated sailors lost at sea. "Remember, it can always get worse!"

"How?" I cried, dropping my head onto the kitchen table. "How can things possibly get any worse than they already are?"

"The espresso machine could break," he replied.

When Zach was younger, the struggle centred on trying to get him to sleep longer than four hours each night. These days, it's become a two-hour marathon just to get him into bed so we can try to get him to sleep longer than four hours each night. At around eighteen months, Zach learned how to climb out of his crib. Despite the practice, his dismount off the railing never improved much past the amateur athlete level, and the landing always ended in tears, usually mine. So we gave up the luxury of forced confinement, packed up the crib, bought a proper bed, low to the ground, and bid a sad farewell to another stage of our baby's life. And then we said hello to a whole new stage of sleeping disorders.

Before Zach was a toddler, and all attempts to get him to fall asleep on his own had failed, I always had the option of nursing or rocking him to sleep. Now, my only recourse—other than the twenty-five different books by his bedside table that I have to, "Do again, Mommy! Again!"—is to kneel beside his bed and pray, "Please God, make him shut his eyes and go to sleep."

The only response I've had so far is "Mommy, who you talking to?"

We have continued with our nighttime ritual like all the experts suggested, but have adjusted it slightly now that Zach is older. His bath now occurs at three p.m. because I've discovered that anything to do with water or bubbles after six only stimulates him. The dinner show starts at five-thirty, starring my melodramatic son as the victim, cringing in horror and crying out, "No! No pasta and carrots!" while Mommy plays the villain, pleading through clenched teeth, "Come on, just open up your mouth. It's not going to kill you!" The short period of quiet play we once indulged in has been replaced by running laps around the living room and dining room in the hopes it might tire him out. Then my husband usually heads up stairs to coax Zach to sleep while I prepare a late dinner for the two of us to enjoy in relative calm. At about nine, I will click the monitor on downstairs to see how much progress my husband has made in the nursery. The broadcast is usually the same: a short slapping sound, followed by, "Wake up, Daddy! Wake up!"

For a while, we reverted back to the controlled crying method, but my heart just wasn't in it. Short of strapping him to the bed, our only option was to close the door firmly behind us, setting off an explosion of screams and tears. I didn't feel like I was training him to sleep on his own. As I listened to him scratch at the door, sniffing and crying out for me, like a lost little puppy that had been left on the side of the road, I felt like I had abandoned him. We tried the Supernanny approach, where you stay in the room, gradually moving further and further away, and patiently put your child back into bed each time he crawls out. After an hour and a half, my patience had long retired and I felt like I was throwing my son back into bed. Of course, Zach thought it was a game, and each night begged for me to do it again. After each different method, I arrived at the same conclusion: that after admitting defeat and lying beside my son for an hour or more to get him to fall asleep, the only way to extract myself from a mattress designed to support a thirty-pound toddler is just to roll straight onto the floor.

We even tried cutting out his afternoon nap—the only hour-and-a-half of sleep he will willingly succumb to if you drive him around in the car long enough. This only created a whole new scary species: the overtired toddler. We pushed his bedtime back to seven-thirty because one expert said, "sleep begets sleep." And so we were reintroduced to the undertired toddler. Daylight savings screwed everything up, so we declared a family bedtime of ten-thirty, which has shortened our bedtime ritual considerably, but there will be hell to pay in October. For the moment, our only course of survival has been to stop hanging out with parents whose children sleep more than six hours, either consecutively, or in spurts.

I was reading a parenting magazine recently that mentioned Dr. Ferber had given an interview with the *New Yorker* magazine in 1999 and had recanted his original position, admitting that some kids were just untrainable. I pointed it out to Andrew: "In 1999!" I said in exasperation. "Why didn't anyone tell us sooner?!"

I took Zach to the park last week and slumped on a bench in an exhausted heap, watching him run around the circumference of the jungle gym for thirty minutes without a break. Another mother whose daughter was playing quietly in the sandbox sat down beside me and commented, "Wow, he has a lot of energy. Did you feed him chocolate or something?"

"No," I replied wearily. "That's just how he is."

"He should sleep well tonight with all this exercise," she said.

"Yes," I sighed. "I thought that once, too."

But my husband is right. We have to remain positive. The espresso machine is still working. Things could be worse.

36

Déjà Baby
Doing It All Over Again

"So, when is number two coming along?" my mother asked the other day. "You need to have at least two children," she told me. "Then you will know one is enough."

"Mom, I can barely handle the child I have now," I said.

"Well, dear," she sighed. "Maybe with two, that wouldn't be so obvious."

I read an article once that said mothers lose brain cells when they give birth; it's nature's way of allowing women to forget the pain of labour so they will be willing to get pregnant again. I would tell you who wrote it, but I can't remember. Besides, I don't think it's childbirth that affects a mother's brain cells. It's more likely the prolonged exposure to the *Teletubbies* and constant recitation of "The Wheels on the Bus Go Round and Round" that does it.

In an attempt to reverse any possible brain damage from childbirth, I briefly considered buying *The Mommy Brain: How Motherhood Makes Us Smarter* by Katherine Ellison. That was until I read the blurb: "Mothers get basic training in the important kinds of smarts as they tone their brain's 'empathy muscles' by instinctively imitating their babies facial expressions." Maybe motherhood has made me smarter. At least I don't need to spend $32.95 to figure out that imitating my son's facial expression when he's filling his diaper would make me look pretty stupid.

Maybe it's the sleep deprivation that destroys brain cells. Yesterday I poured milk on my waffles and put maple syrup in my coffee, and I didn't even notice until I caught myself putting the toaster in the fridge. But I still have enough grey matter left to remember what it felt like when my textbook birth turned into a terrifying tale of the inherent risks of childbirth.

My uterine inversion was, apparently, a one-in-a-million fluke. "You won the lottery," said the specialist I went to see after Zach's birth.

"I would have preferred the 649," I joked. But childbirth is naturally unpredictable—you don't always get to choose your ticket. And while the joy of loving your baby and the passage of time may take the edge off—much like the morphine the doctor gave me in the delivery room—it still doesn't erase the memory of the experience entirely.

It is a testament to the powerful bond of parenthood that a woman would risk her life, or her sanity, to have another baby. When we first started discussing trying for another baby, I told Andrew I wasn't sure if I was ready. "I keep reliving what happened in the delivery room," I said.

"And you think I don't?" he replied softly, and I remembered that, out of the two of us, he had the better front row seat to the whole show.

But, to be honest, my greatest fear about getting pregnant again has nothing to do with labour complications. What really scares me is giving birth to another insomniac, or that a pregnancy will precipitate some other life-altering event—like renovating the house, or moving to another city. Based on the experiences of almost every woman I know who has ever been pregnant, one always seems to follow the other.

Of course, just because we've decided we want to add a third floor to our house doesn't mean it will happen right away. My husband and I know that we got lucky the first time, and we are aware that it may require more than just good aim this time around. There are plenty of obstacles to getting pregnant again—I've read the statistics on the rates of secondary infertility. A news report on the issue had a woman I know so worried she would never have another child that after each time she had sex she stuck her legs in the air and started cycling like she was in the Tour de France. There should have been a news report on the dangers of mixing bicycles with sex. Apparently, all that cycling scrambled her eggs, and now she's having twins.

But for Andrew and me, the exhaustion of already being parents seems to be our main hurdle. The other night, I told him that nudging me awake to let me know that it was now my turn to get up and answer the screams coming from the nursery was not considered foreplay. He replied that rolling over and muttering "fuck you" into my pillow was not considered consummation.

Baby-making may be a labour of love, but it's just like any other job: there are schedules to keep and peer evaluations are held every month based on performance. My husband and I aren't really very ambitious employees. I turn up late and he leaves early, but at least we're dedicated to the task. Of course, any job that is repeated daily runs the risk of turning into a chore—even if you can do it while lying down—so I'm trying to keep it interesting. Last night when Andrew winked at me and said, "How about some baby-making sex tonight?" I suggested spicing things up with some *Gladiator* sex instead. "Gladiator sex?" he asked, his interest obviously piqued—probably imagining something wild and untamed, possibly in an arena. "What's that?"

"Well," I said, "We have sex and I pretend you're Russell Crowe wearing that cute Roman skirt."

I can still remember holding my newborn son in my arms for the very first time, more than two years ago. "I'm a mother," I kept telling myself, and I waited for some grand epiphany about the meaning of life and the importance of family. It never came. The only thing that was clear to me on that particular day was that childbirth was a ridiculous way to introduce someone to the world. But I know now that parenthood is not about one grand epiphany. Being a parent means you experience small epiphanies on a daily basis; those moments when you can feel overwhelming joy, while, at the same time, you struggle with crushing self-doubt and frustration. And as I find myself about to begin this journey again, I watch my son leave his baby days behind him and barrel self-assuredly towards childhood. I wonder if my baby steps will ever turn into such confident strides. The first time I ventured into parenthood I had no idea what I was doing. But I think this time will be different; this time I *know* I have no idea what I'm doing.

I hope you have enjoyed these stories about the roller coaster we call parenthood—the only ride that can make you feel both excited and nauseous, and still have you lining up for another go. And this is where my tales come to an end—for now at least—because I need to concentrate on one job at a time.

And Russell is waiting for me in the bedroom.

—Epilogue—

An Inconceivable Lesson

It's six months after my husband and I started trying for a second baby, and one thing is clear—my husband needs a restraining order. If he comes within three feet of a fertile woman, it will result in a pregnancy. Two miscarriages later, however, and I'm starting to wonder if maybe I should slap my body with a misdemeanour for failing to co-operate with our baby-making plans.

"It's just nature's way," said the doctor after the second miscarriage, which had occurred just three days before I was due to hit that magical twelve-week mark, when the threat of losing the baby is supposed to plummet. "Sometimes these things happen." A battery of tests confirmed the doctor's simple *Chicken Soup for the Soul* diagnosis, but even the fact that as many as 50 percent of pregnancies may end in miscarriage wasn't enough to let me shrug off the loss so easily.

"I want answers!" I cried to my husband. "Or at least an opinion that sounds like it required eight years of medical school to come up with." It would have been a much bigger comfort to have the doctor explain it to me in more clinical terms like, "This anomaly was caused by abnormal fluctuations in the environment, and a misalignment of the cosmos. You must experience three in a row before medical intervention can occur. The only known cure is to try again."

The crash from the pregnancy hormones was like coming off a drug. I was irritable, irrational, emotional and prone to wild snacking binges. My breasts were still sore and full for weeks after, and then suddenly, they disappeared. My stomach, which had swollen to an impressive size during that first trimester, looked like it did shortly after I had given birth to Zach; and unlike my pregnant breasts, the extra rolls of fat I had accumulated in preparation for the new baby refused to disappear.

Six weeks later, my Pap test results came back. "Moderately abnormal," my doctor told me, and at first I thought she was referring to my personality. "It's not cancer," she said, as if that diagnosis was supposed to reassure me that it was okay to have anything abnormal wreaking havoc with my body. "But this is not what caused your miscarriages either," she added, destroying any hope I may have had for a final explanation. My body—which had already proven to have a mind of its own when my uterus inverted during labour—was now obeying about as well as my two-year-old.

Staring into my closet, I declared to my husband that in addition to my pre-pregnancy, pregnancy and post-pregnancy wardrobe, I now needed post-miscarriage clothes, because nothing I owned fit my new in-limbo body shape. I started to slip into a state of self-pity that I wanted to nurture, but with an active and demanding toddler at home, that wasn't a luxury I could afford. I thought of my father, who always asked me, "What can you learn from this experience?" whenever something didn't work out. "That experience is something you get when you didn't get what you wanted," I said out loud, slamming my closet door shut.

It's easy to get caught up in the daily routine of caring for a baby, and forget that you are actually raising a tiny person, one who is constantly listening and absorbing everything around them. Whenever I'm driving alone in the car with my son, I hear the words I normally yell out to his father being mimicked back to me: "Slow down!" "We're going to crash!" "We're lost aren't we?" I walked past the kitchen last week and caught sight of Zach opening the pots and pans drawer in the kitchen. He peered inside and then said, "Hmmm, what will I make for dinner?" Even more surprising than his keen observation of a daily ritual was the fact that he dropped the usual adjective that accompanies that sentence whenever I utter it.

It still amazes me that parents obsess about developing a baby's intelligence. We buy *Baby Einstein* videos, use flashcards, and pay for an endless schedule of ece-approved stimulating activities, when really, a baby doesn't appear to need any extra help to learn about how life unfolds around him. Zach was grocery shopping with Andrew recently, and as they walked through the aisles Zach began to ask for cookies, toys and anything else that was within his three-foot-high line of sight. In a clever bid to try and avoid a public tantrum, Andrew responded to each request with the query, "Do you have any money? Because you need money to buy all those things," leaving the would-be consumer quietly stumped. At the end of their trip, Andrew strapped Zach— who had emerged from the store, sadly empty-handed—into his car seat. "Daddy," he sighed, "I need to buy some money."

Not once have I ever mentioned or explained to my son why I stop at the gas station to fill the car up. And yet, the last time we went to the toddler drop-in gym, I watched Zach zoom around in one of the gym's Little Tykes pick-up trucks. He stopped his ride to drag one of the play gas pumps over and pretended to fill up the truck's gas tank. He repeated the whole ceremony about three times before he eventually got impatient, threw the nozzle down, picked up the pump, tossed it in the back of the pick-up truck, climbed in and pedalled away.

Impressive, I thought. He may only be two, but he's still old enough to know the price of gas is ridiculous.

I was sitting at the dinner table the other night when Zach walked up to me and put his head on my lap, "Is your belly still sore, Mommy?" he asked. "I kiss it and make it better?" We hadn't fully explained to him what had happened, but the drama around him—the doctor's appointments, and my crying fits on the couch—had obviously left an impression.

"No, sweetie. Mommy's belly isn't sore anymore, just her heart," I replied, tapping my chest. He climbed up and planted a loud smack where my hand had just been. Then he jumped down and ran back to play with his train set, as if that one kiss had settled the matter.

I realized that with everything my son is learning from me, and my husband, and the people around him, I have picked up surprisingly little from him. Apparently, children laugh up to two hundred times a day, while adults only laugh up to twenty. Some days, it's even less. To my son, everything can be turned into a game. Whenever I start heading towards the computer to do some work, he rushes over and giggles, "Sit by the computer, Mommy, and I'll bother you." What I find irritating, he considers it quality time. I have watched him, without provocation or enticement, suddenly jump up and run around in circles, alive with laughter. He can extract such pure joy from any moment, for no reason other than the simple fact that he is able to do so.

The doctor called the other day. Further tests had confirmed that "moderately abnormal" had been downgraded to "mildly insane." This time I knew she was talking about my personality. Baby-making can, once again, resume. Feeling positive for the first time in over two months I went to pick Zach up from his morning at Play School. He ran out of the room towards me, smiling as he pleaded, "Ice cream! Ice cream!"

I started my usual reply, "Sorry honey, it's lunch time now, we can't have ice cream." Then, I stopped myself. Why can't we? I thought. Ice cream could be considered a food group. Would his development into a successful, well-adjusted, intelligent adult— the sort who would support his mother in her old age—really be irretrievably altered if we skipped lunch this once and had ice cream instead? "Let's go get some ice cream," I said reaching for his hand.

Later, as we sat together on a bench, happily licking our ice cream cones in the sun, it occurred to me that the years I have my son all to myself—before school, friends, soccer games and first loves take over—are so fleeting that I'm sure I will soon look back and wonder if they ever even existed at all. Life is short. Sometimes it ends before it even gets a chance to begin. And for once I just sat there. I didn't worry if I was being a good enough mother, or if my son was being properly stimulated. For once, I took a cue from my son and just enjoyed the moment, even as he smeared his little chocolate-covered hands all over the one pair of pants I could still fit into.

Baby may be a four-letter word. But then, so is love.